INTRODUCTION TO LUCRETIUS

T0382168

INTRODUCTION TO
LUCRETIUS

by

A. P. SINKER, M.A.

CAMBRIDGE

AT THE UNIVERSITY PRESS

1967

CAMBRIDGE UNIVERSITY PRESS
Cambridge, New York, Melbourne, Madrid, Cape Town,
Singapore, São Paulo, Delhi, Mexico City

Cambridge University Press
The Edinburgh Building, Cambridge CB2 8RU, UK

Published in the United States of America by Cambridge University Press, New York

www.cambridge.org
Information on this title: www.cambridge.org/9781107621183

First edition 1937
First published 1937
Reprinted 1962, 1967
Re-issued 2013

A catalogue record for this publication is available from the British Library

ISBN 978-1-107-62118-3 Paperback

CONTENTS

PREFACE

As the mass of the world's literature grows greater we are more and more subjected to the temptation to take it in tabloid form. Anthologies become a menace. An apology is needed for a book which may appear to add to the menace.

The book has three main objects. (1) It is intended to be not an alternative but an introduction to a full reading of the *de Rerum Natura*. In order to read any part of the *de R.N.* with full appreciation it is necessary to have a knowledge of the whole, since all the parts are mutually inter-dependent. "To the general reader what will come home most is the spirit of the whole, the problems with which Lucretius is faced and the general attitude in which he goes to meet them. *And if one is to appreciate this fully, it is more than all else necessary to have the clear conception of the main principles and their fearless application.*"[1] My own introduction to Lucretius consisted in reading the fifth book by itself, and much of it left me puzzled and unappreciative until, years later, I read the whole poem. The sentence in italics above suggested to me that a better way to approach Lucretius for the first time would be to read him in such a way that an understanding of the structure of the whole poem and of Lucretius' "world-outlook" should be obtained. Once this is done it should be possible to read any part of the poem with a proper realisation of its relation to the whole.

(2) For those who no longer need an introduction to the *de R.N.* but who intend to read or re-read parts of it, or the whole, I hope that the book may be a

---

[1] C. Bailey, *Transl. of Lucretius*, intro. p. 21 : italics mine.

convenience as a kind of Baedeker to the intricacies
of the structure of the poem and of the system of
philosophy which it embodies. It gives a small-scale
map of the whole wood which may be useful for
reference when the traveller is involved in any particular group of trees.

(3) A systematic account of the *de R.N.* is necessarily also a systematic account of Epicureanism. It
is doubtful whether a professional philosopher would
consider a study of Epicureanism—the philosophy of
the plain man and definitely not that of the professional philosopher—a desirable introduction to the
study of philosophy in general. But Epicureanism at
least raises some of the fundamental problems of
philosophy, and to this extent may serve as an introduction to more advanced philosophic thought.—A
word of warning is necessary about the way in which
Epicureanism is here presented. For the sake of
brevity I have had to treat it as though it were a
skeleton instead of a living organism. It is presented
as a closed and rigid system, whereas in reality it is
a stage in the organic growth of a certain line of
thought. I have had to omit nearly all reference both
to the previous philosophers to whom Epicurus owed
much and to the subsequent philosophers who have
owed much to Epicureanism.

The method adopted has been to select from the
de R.N. a number of passages, the total length of
which is about equal to the fifth book, and to arrange
them in such a way that they make clear the main
features of the Epicurean system. In the selected
passages there is, I think, a fair proportion both of
" honey " and of " wormwood ". In the second section

of the systematic account of Epicureanism, namely
Natural Science, I have followed exactly the arrangement and sub-divisions of the *de R.N.*, and in so
doing I have tried to elucidate the structure of the
poem.

The selected passages are connected by summaries
and by a running commentary, a method suggested
by that used in a recent book by Prof. F. M. Cornford,
who writes, "It is not clear why we should be forced
to read a book in three places at once." In the present
book the three places have only been reduced to two,
the linguistic notes on the text appearing as usual at
the end. These notes have been made as brief as
possible and I have aimed at elucidating the meaning
rather than at imparting grammatical and syntactical
information.

The text is that of Dr Cyril Bailey (Oxf. Text,
2nd ed.), which I have followed throughout except
in four places. Once I have omitted a comma, and
in the other three places I have avoided obeli by
adopting admittedly uncertain emendations (VI. 713;
III. 84, 962; IV. 79). There is no critical "apparatus",
because the primary aim of the book is to give an idea
of the *de R.N.* as a whole and for this an "apparatus"
is unnecessary, however useful in gaining a detailed
understanding.

For the rest of the book—almost as much as for
the text—I am indebted to Dr Bailey above all. His
prose translation of Lucretius is frequently (though
not invariably) quoted in the following pages. To anyone who has studied his *Greek Atomists and Epicurus*
my debt to this book also will be only too obvious
throughout the running commentary. "Epicurus
expresses in words what he wishes to say and states

clearly what I can understand", says the Epicurean
in Cicero's dialogue *de Finibus*, and whether this be
true or not of Epicurus it is certainly true of his
modern expositor. After Dr Bailey, I have relied
chiefly on the great editions of the *de R.N.* by Munro
and by Giussani, but I am also much indebted to the
useful collection of material in Merrill's edition and to
the school editions of Books I, III, v by Mr J. D. Duff.
Other books which have been of special help are
noted in the select bibliography.

Thanks to these, I have found that closer ac-
quaintance with Lucretius has given me ever greater
pleasure in his poetry, and I hope that some of the
enjoyment that has accompanied the making of this
book may pass on to those who use it. The problems
dealt with in the *de R.N.* are problems that enter into
the experience of the human being almost as soon as
he can begin to think—the problem of the nature of
the universe, of the meaning if any that inspires it,
above all the problem of death. To his treatment of
these themes Lucretius brings a passionate intensity
of feeling, a capacity for detailed observation and for
the conception of vivid analogies, and a magnificent
command of language and of rhythm. He is a poet
whose poetry can thrill the young equally with the
middle-aged—a quality that is not I think shared by
the Augustan poets; and he is a poet whose inner
conflict is widely reflected in the minds of the present
generation.

I wish to thank Mr F. H. Sandbach, Fellow of
Trinity College, who has very kindly read the introduction and running commentary in proof. His care
and penetration have reduced the number of places

where looseness of thought or inaccuracy of expression is evident; though I am conscious that precision in matters of detail has sometimes had to be sacrificed to the requirements of conciseness or of simplicity. I owe a debt of gratitude too for very helpful suggestions made from time to time both by pupils with whom I have read Lucretius and by my wife.

A. P. S.

Jesus College, Cambridge
February 1937

ἡ τετραφάρμακος·
ἄφοβον ὁ θεός, ἀναίσθητον ὁ θάνατος, καὶ τἀγαθὸν
μὲν εὔκτητον, τὸ δὲ δεινὸν εὐεκκαρτέρητον.[1]

The Four-fold Cure.

In God there is nothing to fear,
In Death there is nothing to feel;
What is good is easily won,
What is ill is easily borne.

---

[1] This summary of Epicurean moral teaching is quoted
by Bailey, *Epicurus*, p. 347.

LIST OF SELECTED PASSAGES
from the *de Rerum Natura*

de R.N.	Order in this book
I. 50–135	1
136–145	21
418–482	5
921–950	2
951–983	6
II. 1–33	17
216–293	7
333–407	8*
1090–1104	16
III. 14–24	15
59–93	20
94–160	9
231–322	10*
830–977	19
IV. 26–109	11
379–521	3
V. 146–155	14
564–591	12*
925–1240	13
VI. 58–79	18
703–737	4*

If the selected passages are found to be too many it is suggested that those marked with an asterisk be the first to be omitted.

SELECT BIBLIOGRAPHY
AND LIST OF ABBREVIATIONS

Andrade   Prof. E. N. da C. Andrade, intro. (*The Scientific Significance of Lucretius*) to Munro's Comm. (1928).

B.   Dr Cyril Bailey, *The Greek Atomists and Epicurus* (1928) (cf. review by A. E. Taylor, *Classical Review*, XLIII, 2).

B. tr.   —— Transl. of *de R.N.* (1924).

B. Oxf. T. —— Oxford Text of *de R.N.* 2nd ed. (1921).

B. Epic.   —— *Epicurus* (extant remains), text, transl., comm.

Davies   H. S. Davies, "Notes on Lucretius", in *Criterion* for Oct. 1931.

Duff   J. D. Duff, comm. Books I, III, V.

Giuss.   C. Giussani, intro. studies and comm. (Italian, ed. 1923–4).

Guyau   J.-M. Guyau, *La Morale d'Épicure*.

M.   H. A. J. Munro, comm. (final (fourth) ed.).

Merrill   W. A. Merrill, comm. (1906).

Sikes   E. E. Sikes, *Lucretius, Poet and Philosopher* (1936).

INTRODUCTION

(i) (a) HISTORICAL BACKGROUND OF EPICURUS AND OF LUCRETIUS

When towards the end of the fifth century B.C. philosophers began to turn their thoughts from Natural
Science to Ethics, Greek city-states still enjoyed political freedom. With Socrates and Plato, therefore, the
moral duty of man as an individual is inseparable from
his moral duty as a citizen. Aristotle's ethical views
followed, rather belatedly, the same tradition. But with
the rise of Macedonia in the middle of the fourth
century the Greek city-state declined from a position
of independence to a position of subordination in a
military empire. The inhabitants of Greek cities ceased
to have duties and responsibilities as citizens and found
themselves forced to act under orders from Macedonia.
The problem, How should a good citizen behave?
ceased to have any meaning.

Epicurus was born in 341 B.C. and never knew political freedom. His philosophy was conditioned by the
political circumstances of the period. First, he is not
concerned with the moral duty of man as a citizen but
only with the moral duty of man as an individual.
Second, his philosophy betrays the uncertainty and lack
of confidence of an age following a great disaster—the
disaster of the Macedonian conquest of Greece. The
motto of all his moral teaching might well be "Safety
First". "Philosophy is no longer the pillar of fire going
before a few intrepid seekers after truth: it is rather an
ambulance following in the wake of the struggle for
existence and picking up the weak and wounded."[1]

The political circumstances which conditioned Epicureanism at its birth were to some extent reproduced
in the time of Lucretius. Political freedom, and the

[1] C. F. Angus, *Cambridge Anc. Hist.* VII, 231.

duties and responsibilities of man as a citizen, were beginning to disappear at Rome just as they had disappeared at Athens. The republic had been shaken to its foundations and despotism was looming near Public life was ceasing to be the natural occupation of the educated class. It was at this time therefore that Epicureanism and Stoicism, the philosophies of man as an individual, began to make an especially strong appeal at Rome. The *de R.N.*, in which the Epicurean system of Natural Science is set forth, is a symptom of the beginning of the downfall of the Roman republic.

(i) (b) Epicurus

Epicurus (b. 341 B.C.) spent his childhood in Samos, his father having gone there as a colonist from Athens. His early manhood was spent in the cities of Asia Minor, where he studied philosophy. In 307 he settled in Athens, at that time under the domination of Demetrius Poliorcetes, and bought a house between the city and the Peiraeus. His house and the famous Garden became the centre of a kind of Society of Friends, and for thirty-seven years Epicurus lived in retirement as their leader. Most unusually by Greek standards, even women and slaves were admitted on terms of friendship. Epicurus died at the age of seventy.

From what we know of Epicurus' relationships with other members of the community, his character was marked by exceptional gentleness and humanity. The life of the community was frugal: luxury was not connected with Epicureanism till long after. Epicurus was a voluminous writer, and his writings were held in the greatest reverence by his followers; so much so that no changes were subsequently made in his teaching, and there was never a school of "Neo-Epicureans" (as, for instance, of Neo-Platonists). Lucretius in the *de R.N.* never departs from his master's doctrines.

(i) (c) TITUS LUCRETIUS CARUS

About the life of Lucretius we have hardly any certain knowledge. He was born between the years 100 and 94 B.C. and died probably in 55 or 54 B.C. His poem was published at his death in the unfinished state in which he left it. Cicero may have been the editor of it.

In the *de R.N.* Lucretius tells us practically nothing about himself.[1] The tone of equality which he adopts towards Memmius makes it fairly certain that he was a Roman aristocrat; though it is clear that he did not take part in public life. The story that he wrote the poem in the lucid intervals of a madness brought on by a love-potion and that he finally committed suicide,[2] recorded by Jerome (fourth century A.D.), is perhaps an invention due to early Christian hostility towards the supposed atheist. Of more interest than Jerome's piece of scandal is the passage in Virgil's second Georgic referring to Lucretius, which might well serve him for an epitaph:

> felix, qui potuit rerum cognoscere causas
> atque metus omnes et inexorabile fatum
> subiecit pedibus strepitumque Acherontis avari.[3]

(i) (d) GAIUS MEMMIUS

The *de R.N.* is addressed to Memmius and Lucretius claims him as a friend, but he seems to have been unworthy of Lucretius' friendship. Catullus gives him a black character in his tenth and twenty-eighth poems, and his political career was one of treachery and finally

[1] For suggestions about his character arising out of the poem see sect. (ii) of the Introduction.
[2] See Tennyson's poem, "Lucretius".
[3] G. II. 490–492.

(after Lucretius' death) disgrace. His interest in Epicureanism must have been very slight, for we learn
from a letter written by Cicero to him (*ad Fam.* XIII. 1)
that he had bought in Athens a piece of ground on
which were ruins of Epicurus' own house and that he
refused to give it up to the contemporary head of the
Epicurean school and his followers, who no doubt
viewed the ground as a holy place.

(ii) "L'ANTI-LUCRÈCE CHEZ LUCRÈCE"[1]

"Art for Art's sake" is a formula which finds less support now than a generation or two ago. In the revolt
against the moral uplift which characterized much of
the art and literature of the last century the pendulum
swung too far. A less extreme view finds more favour
now, which might be expressed in the formula—if a
formula is wanted—"Art for Life's sake". We no
longer altogether rule out the view of Aristophanes and
Sir Philip Sidney that the function of poetry is to teach
Virtue (though "Life" in our formula and "Virtue"
in theirs may not be synonymous). We no longer view
the phrase "didactic poetry" as a contradiction in
terms. But the fact remains that didactic poetry which
is also good poetry is extremely rare. What then are
the special difficulties or dangers besetting didactic
poetry?

It is not easy to answer this question in a few lines,
but if we attempt to do so we might put our answer as
follows.—The poet who wishes to convey instruction,
the didactic poet, is likely to have his attention fixed
at least as much upon his readers as upon the ideas that
he is trying to express, and this distraction of the poet's
attention from his theme to his audience is more likely
to produce rhetoric than poetry. Keats voiced the

---

[1] The phrase or Patin, *Études sur la poésie latine.*

feeling of everyone when he said that he disliked a
poet who had "a palpable design" upon the reader,
and in didactic poetry the design is only too apt to
show through. There is no great poetry that is not
passionately sincere expression of the poet's inner experience, and where the poet's attention is too much
diverted from his own inner experience to his audience
he is likely to fail.

There are many poems, e.g. the *Aeneid*, about which
we might reasonably hesitate if we were asked to say
whether they can be classed as didactic poetry or not;
but there can be no doubt about the *de R.N.* How far
then does it escape the blight that lies on most didactic
poetry?

Anyone who reads the *de R.N.* is bound to be im-
pressed by the passionate intensity and sincerity of
Lucretius' tone. He writes with a passion strangely at
variance with the passionless state of mind that he
advocates as man's true ideal. He writes with a depth
of conviction that is not easily reached without a profound inner conflict. It may help to an appreciation
of Lucretius if we pause for a moment to consider some
of the passages where the signs of this conflict are most
evident.

Towards the end of the third book, after an accumulation of twenty-eight proofs of the mortality of the soul,
comes the line that is the climax of the *de R.N.*:

Nil igitur mors est ad nos neque pertinet hilum.

It is followed by one of the finest passages in the poem,
in which Lucretius holds up to scorn the folly of the
fear of death. But, for all his scorn, the most moving
lines are those beginning,

Iam iam non domus accipiet te laeta...

which are put into the mouth of an imaginary *opponent*

—an opponent who points out that, though death may
hold no torments in store for us, yet the mere thought
of the cessation of the joys of life gives cause enough
for fear of death. Lucretius answers his opponent with
the voice of reason, but it is difficult not to feel that
his heart is with his opponent, or rather that it is his
own heart speaking on the other side in opposition to
his head. In the preceding paragraph Lucretius has
been describing the man who professes a belief in the
mortality of the soul *without sincerely holding it.* "*You*
may be sure that his words do not ring true and that
there lurks in his heart a secret goad, though he himself declare that he does not believe that any sense will
remain to him after death." *Subesse caecum aliquem
cordi stimulum* is a self-revealing phrase, and in the
iam iam non domus lines Lucretius shows that he himself
was not entirely free from the prickings of a *caecus
stimulus.* An intense love of life, such as is evident
throughout the *de R.N.*, is incompatible with entire
equanimity in the contemplation of death, however
clearly reason may argue that death is annihilation and
that (in Lucretius' words) "there abides with thee no
longer any yearning for these things". Claudio's words
in *Measure for Measure* illustrate better than any description the nature of the inner conflict that we may
suspect in Lucretius. When Isabella first hints to
Claudio that he is to be put to death, his reception of
the news would have had the full approval of Lucretius
the philosopher:

> If I must die,
> I will encounter darkness as a bride,
> And hug it in mine arms.

We are reminded of the more staid simile used by
Lucretius himself: "Why dost thou not retire like a
guest sated with the banquet of life, and with calm
mind embrace, thou fool, a rest that knows no care?"

But later in the same scene, Claudio lifts the veil and
lets us see the other side of the inner conflict:

> Ay, but to die, and go we know not where;
> To lie in cold obstruction and to rot;
> This sensible warm motion to become
> A kneaded clod;...
> To be imprison'd in the viewless winds,
> And blown with restless violence round about
> The pendent world; or to be worse than worst
> Of those that lawless and incertain thought
> Imagine howling: 'tis too horrible!

By giving us the two passages within a few lines of
each other, Shakespeare shows how these two opposing
states of mind can exist side by side. It would be an
exaggeration to suggest that Lucretius was as much
torn between the two as Claudio, or that his *nil igitur
mors est ad nos* does not ring true. But it is not un-
reasonable to attribute the intensity of his feeling on
the subject of Death to an inner struggle in which his
head did not win an easy victory over his heart.[1]

There are other passages in the *de R.N.* which suggest a similar conflict between Lucretius the poet and
Lucretius the philosopher. Lucretius as philosopher
held the orthodox Epicurean belief that the sun and
moon are about the size they appear to be, namely the
size of not very large rocks, and that they are at no
great distance from the earth. These orthodox theories
are set forth in a matter-of-fact way in the course of
the fifth book.[2] Later on in the same book we come
to a passage the tone of which seems strangely inconsistent with this belief, and the poetic fire of the passage
tells us that Lucretius is again writing with his heart
rather than with his head. The passage begins: "For

[1] Lucr. III, esp. ll. 830–977 (Passage 19); Shakespeare,
M. for M. Act III, Sc. i.

[2] v. 564–591 (Passage 12). Similarly the stars were held
by the Epicureans to be mere pin-points of light.

when we turn our gaze on the heavenly quarters of the great upper world, and ether fast above the glittering stars, and direct our thoughts to the courses of the sun and moon, then into our breasts burdened with other ills that fear as well begins to exalt its re-awakened head, the fear that we may haply find the power of the gods to be unlimited, able to wheel the bright stars in their varied motion." This feeling of awe, natural to the poet in the presence of the immensity of the starry heavens, is strange in a philosopher who reduced the heavens to so petty a scale. He then proceeds to speak of the might of nature's forces and the powerlessness of man:

> usque adeo res humanas vis abdita quaedam
> obterit.

The phrase *vis abdita quaedam* reminds us of the *caecus stimulus* in Book III, and suggests that here too the imagination of the poet hinted at things beyond the range of the reasoning of the philosopher.[1]

Perhaps it is a truism to say that great poetry is more often than not the product of an intense inner conflict in the poet; but it may be worth while to cite the testimony of poets themselves. Lucretius' own contemporary, Catullus, illustrates the inner conflict in one of its commonest forms in literature:

> Odi et amo. Quare id faciam, fortasse requiris.
> Nescio, sed fieri sentio et excrucior.

A closer parallel with Lucretius may be found in Milton. Another great poet, Blake, wrote of *Paradise Lost* as follows:

The reason Milton wrote in fetters when he wrote of Angels and God, and at liberty when of Devils and Hell, is because he was a true Poet, and of the Devil's party without knowing it.

---

[1] v. 1204–1240 (Passage 13); and cf. VI. 58 ff. (Passage 18). For further illustration and discussion of the conflict between Lucretius the philosopher and Lucretius the poet refer to Index, *s.v.* "L'anti-Lucrèce".

In *Paradise Lost*, and in Milton himself, we see a conflict between, on the one side, Reason, order, sublime
tranquillity; on the other side, Passion, heroic energy,
unsatisfied desire that strives for ever after the un-
attainable and is never at rest. In Lucretius Philosophy
won, perhaps, a more complete victory than did Religion in Milton, but otherwise the nature of the conflict
in the two poets is very similar.—A modern poet,
W. B. Yeats, analysing the nature of his own inspira-
tion, writes thus of his attempts to write poetry which
shall express *himself* and not the conflict in himself:

> When I shut my door and light the candle, I invite a
> Marmorean Muse, an art, where no thought or emotion has
> come to mind because another man has thought or felt
> something different, for now there must be no reaction,
> action only, and the world must move my heart but to
> the heart's discovery of itself,...: all my thoughts have ease
> and joy, I am all virtue and confidence. When I come to
> put in rhyme what I have found it will be a hard toil, but
> for a moment I believe I have found myself and not my
> anti-self. It is only the shrinking from toil perhaps that
> convinces me that I have been no more myself than is the
> cat the medicinal grass it is eating in the garden.

This calls to mind the pregnant phrase used by the
French critic, "l'anti-Lucrèce chez Lucrèce". Epicureanism was to some extent Lucretius' "medicinal
grass", and both "self" and "anti-self" find expression
in the *de R.N.*[1]

Epicurus has been called "the most humane and
gentle among the ancients". His whole system of
philosophy is, so far as we can tell, a reflection of his
temperament. Blest with a contented and cheerful disposition and with an exceptional gift for making and

---

[1] Catullus, 85; Blake, *Marriage of Heaven and Hell*;
Yeats, *Essays*, p. 485. Yeats' later poems constantly give
expression to this inner conflict, e.g. "*Ego Dominus Tuus*",
"Sailing to Byzantium", "A Dialogue of Self and Soul"
(*Collected Poems*, pp. 180, 217, 265).

keeping friends, he appears to us as one of those fortunate beings whose natural gifts coincide with their ideals. He was born an Epicurean. About Lucretius' character we know little except what we can gather from his work, but the contrast between him and Epicurus is clear enough. The *de R.N.* suggests that the writer was of a sombre and on the whole pessimistic disposition, and that passion and anxiety played a large part in his life. It is noticeable that he has practically nothing to say on the theme of friendship, which occupied such an important part in Epicurus' own teaching.[1] Thus in temperament he was totally unlike Epicurus, but, as so often happens, he felt the attraction of the opposite and he seized on the philosophy which offered the tranquillity of mind that he so much lacked.

We may well conclude that the anxious and passionate missionary spirit that is evident throughout the *de R.N.* is due not so much to a disinterested wish to instruct Memmius, nor even to a wish to convert mankind, as to Lucretius' desire to force *himself* to the mould of the master who was so different from him. In this we may see the explanation why the *de R.N.* escapes the blight that lies on most didactic poetry. "A palpable design" on his reader is not uppermost in Lucretius' mind: his eye is directed not so much outward towards his audience as inward towards the conflict experienced in his own mind. And because the problems with which he deals—the nature of the universe, the question of a divine providence, and, above all, the question of death—are problems which arouse a similar conflict to a greater or less degree in the mind of every man, we are still moved by the poem in which Lucretius attempted to resolve the conflict.

[1] See pp. 100, 101.

(iii) Language and Metre

Lucreti poemata ut scribis ita sunt, multis luminibus ingeni, multae tamen artis. Cic. *ad Q. frat.* II. 11 (9).

(*a*) Language

The only great poem written in Latin hexameters before the time of Lucretius was the *Annals* of Ennius.[1] Lucretius gives his predecessor ungrudging praise. "Our own Ennius, who first bore down from pleasant Helicon the wreath of deathless leaves, to win bright fame among the tribes of Italian peoples."[2] Amongst the Roman poets contemporary with Lucretius, of whom Catullus was of course chief, it was the fashion to despise Ennius for his ruggedness and to admire the Alexandrian school of Greek poets; elegance rather than grandeur was the fashionable literary virtue. Cicero and Lucretius both stood apart from this contemporary movement. Cicero spoke with disdain of the fashionable poets as "cantores Euphorionis", Euphorion being an erudite Alexandrian poet and grammarian. Lucretius wrote in a consciously archaic style, which was suitable to the grandeur of his theme and, incidentally, showed his admiration for Ennius. His praise of Ennius, quoted above, is intentionally reminiscent of Ennius' own words. *Per gentes Italas hominum quae clara clueret* recalls Ennius' *nostra Latinos | per populos terrasque poemata clara cluebunt*; the use of the archaic verb *cluere*[3] being especially significant.

Some of the linguistic forms used by Lucretius are puzzling at first sight to a reader accustomed to classical

[1] The main fragments of Ennius' verse are given in the *Oxford Book of Latin Verse*.

[2] I. 117–119.

[3] See n. on I. 119 (Passage 1).

Latin. There follows a list of examples of some of the more common of these.

(1) Case-endings:

Gen. sing.: *aquāī, animāī, materiāī.*

Abl. sing.: *marĕ* (for *mari*); *parti, nubi* (for *parte, nube*); *quique* (for *quoque*).

Gen. plur.: *Molossum, consanguineum.*

(2) Forms of verbs:

Infin. pass.: *cunctariĕr, cohiberier, volvier* (for *cunctari, cohiberi, volvi*).

Transferred conjugation: *tuĭmur, cĭmus* (*tuēmur, ciēmus* are the classical Latin forms).

potis est (= *potest*). *siet* and *fuat* (both = *sit*).

Contraction: *protraxe* (*protraxisse*), *consumpse* (*consumpsisse*); *irritāt* (*irritavit*).

(3) Preposition:

indu = in. Also *indugredi, indupediri*, etc.

(4) Unusual order of words (mainly for metrical convenience):

Tmesis: *seiungi seque gregari, qui vitam cumque....*

Reversed order: *quibus e.*

Lucretius uses also a considerable number of words which are peculiar to him among good writers. Of these coinages some are due to the nature of the subject: he manufactured the word *clīnamen*, for instance, to express the "swerve" of the atoms. Others are due to metrical necessity or convenience: for instance, *variantia* and *dispositūras* in place of the metrically impossible *vărĭĕtas* and *dispŏsĭtĭones*. The most interesting type of unusual word employed by Lucretius is the compound adjective. Early Roman poets had followed the Greek practice and had freely coined compound adjectives. Both Lucretius and Catullus followed their example. *Terriloquus, fluctifragus, velivolus, horri-*

sonus, noctivagus, levisomnus, perterricrepus are a few
of the many examples in the *de R.N.* To our ears such
words seem pictorially effective and add much to the
vividness of Lucretius' descriptive passages. But, for
some reason which we are unable to appreciate, the
Romans of the succeeding generation found them dis-
tasteful. The Augustan poets employed them but rarely
and confined themselves to simple compounds such as
armiger, omnipotens.

Lucretius' syntax is sometimes unusual. It is well
to remember that *constructio ad sensum* is a favourite of
his. Most difficulties can be resolved if we look to the
meaning rather than to rigid syntactic rules.

In Latin, as probably in most languages, alliteration
and assonance appear frequently from the earliest times.
In the extant fragments of Ennius there are many
striking examples. One of the most striking is from
his tragedy *Andromache*:

> Haec omnia vidi inflammari,
> Priamo vi vitam evitari,
> Iovis aram sanguine turpari.

Amongst subsequent writers, Lucretius is remarkable
for his fondness for alliteration and assonance. Sometimes he uses them in such a way that the sound reflects
the sense of the words; sometimes he evidently takes
a pleasure in the sound purely for its own sake. Memorable examples are, *vivida vis animi pervicit*; *flammantia
moenia mundi*; *venti vis verberat*; *mortalem vitam mors
cum immortalis ademit*. Alliteration and assonance are
so frequent that they colour the whole poem and are
an outstanding feature of Lucretian music. In the
notes on the text I have not drawn attention to individual
examples. The best way to read Latin poetry is to read
it aloud: when this is not possible, the attentive reader
will still read with his mental ears open; and in either
case the effect of alliteration and assonance will be felt

without a running accompaniment of exclamations from the editor.

Prosaic passages and phrases are another characteristic of the *de R.N.*: from the nature of the subject it was inevitable that this should be so. Lucretius, however, often seems to us surprisingly careless on this point, until we remember that the line of demarcation between "prosaic" and "poetic" constantly shifts. When Ennius wrote in his *Annals*,

> septingenti sunt paulo plus aut minus anni
> augusto augurio postquam incluta condita Roma est,

the dry record of historical facts had not come to be thought of as more suitable for prose. Similarly, when Lucretius wrote,

> id quod iam supera tibi paulo ostendimus ante,[1]

the proper use of footnotes had not been invented. There are arid passages of scientific exposition, but we can rarely read far without coming across an oasis— some vividly descriptive word, or a metaphor that suggests the oneness of all things both living and inanimate, for instance *flammai flos*. When so many Latin metaphors have passed on into English and have long ago been worked to death, it is particularly difficult for us to recapture the freshness of many of Lucretius' metaphors: *concilium*, for instance, applied to inanimate objects is properly a metaphor (the word is used in this way by Lucretius only amongst good Latin writers); but its metaphorical force is easily lost on us, for we are hardly conscious of any metaphor at all in the English phrase "concourse of atoms". The more that the reader can forget his English insensitivity to metaphor, the less likely he is to complain that the scientific parts of the *de R.N.* are prosaic.[2]

[1] I. 429.
[2] For Lucretius' use of metaphor see p. 36, n. 1.

(iii) (b) METRE

There is no space here to enter into the interesting question of the development of the Latin hexameter,[1] and without doing so it is impossible to give any coherent account of the metre of Lucretius. A few general remarks, therefore, and the enumeration of a few details will have to suffice.

First, the individual line. Lucretius differs from Virgil most markedly in the following points.[2] There is frequently a diaeresis at the end of the second foot, e.g. *omnia denique sancta, at primordia gignundis.* The fourth foot is often contained in a word, e.g. *tibi suavis daedala tellus,* where Virgil would probably have preferred *suavis tibi.* The fifth and sixth feet are not subject to the Virgilian rules: endings such as *materiai, mente animoque, quandoquidem extat, securum agere aevom, constare: id ita esse* are not at all uncommon. Lucretius' elisions are often awkward, as some of the examples just quoted show. Most of the differences so far enumerated between the practice of Lucretius and the practice of Virgil can be explained by the general statement that Lucretius did not possess Virgil's subtlety in handling the two counterpoised forces which together produce the music of the hexameter, word-accent and metrical ictus.

Second, the structure of groups of lines. In Latin hexameter poetry before Virgil there was a strong tendency to make the end of a clause coincide with the end of the line. An outstanding example of this is provided by the extant fragment of Cicero's *de Con-*

[1] For an excellent introduction to this subject see W. R. Hardie, *Res Metrica,* pp. 196 ff., "The History of Metre at Rome".

[2] The examples in this paragraph are taken from M. pp. 13, 14.

sulatu Suo,[1] which is mostly written in clauses of stock
length; and thus we even get rhyme, through the
recurrence of verbs at the end of lines. Lucretius'
lines are not quite so frequently "end-stopped" as
Cicero's, but they are far more so than Virgil's, as a
comparison of any two passages selected at random will
show. Virgil had the art—indeed he invented the art—
of varying the structure of groups of hexameter lines
in such a way that he was able to produce endlessly
different patterns of sound. The lines of Lucretius
march past us like soldiers in ordered ranks. The lines
of Virgil are more like a kind of processional dance,
where the dancers move past, in groups of varying size,
to a tempo that is constantly varying. But, although
Virgil's method is the more subtle, the method of
Lucretius is admirably suited to his subject. The
cumulative effect of Lucretius' lines intensifies the
cumulative effect of the arguments that he advances,
as for instance when he gives us with relentless per-
sistence a succession of twenty-eight proofs of the
mortality of the soul. The rhythmical subtlety of Virgil
would be out of place here. Changing the former simile,
we may say that Lucretius' lines are like a long flight
of steps, and each line or compact group of lines carries
us a step forward in the argument.

    Third, prosody. A few points may be collected under
this heading which might cause difficulty. Quantity
sometimes varies, e.g. *lĭquidus* and *līquidŭs*, *cŭpido* and
cuppedo, *rēī* and *rĕī*, *sūādet* and *sŭadet*, *tĕnuis* and *tĕnŭis*.
Final *s* is often disregarded, as it was by earlier poets,
e.g. *privatu' doloribus aegris*. *-que* is sometimes added
to a word ending in short *e*, e.g. *mutareque*.

---

[1] *Oxford Book of Latin Verse*, no. 55.

TEXT
AND RUNNING COMMENTARY

LUCRETIUS' PURPOSE

In the following passage Lucretius introduces us to the main purpose of the *de Rerum Natura*.

His avowed purpose is to show the way to the ideal life, to that state of ἀταραξία, tranquillity of mind, which was the aim of Epicurus. Mankind is faced with two great obstacles to the achievement of peace of mind, first, fear of the gods, and second, fear of death. The only way to surmount these obstacles is to gain an understanding of the true nature of things, for this understanding will show, first, that everything is attributable to a natural, nothing to a supernatural, cause, and second, that the soul is mortal and therefore death can hold no horrors in store for us. It is with this practical object in view—the removal of fear—that Lucretius embarks on his exposition of Natural Science.

In the first paragraph (50–61) he mentions the physical basis on which the whole Epicurean system is founded, namely the atoms, *primordia rerum*.

He then branches off to speak of the two foes to man's peace of mind. First (62–101) he tells how Epicurus vanquished religion and indicates the monstrous crimes of which religion is guilty. Second (102–126) he shows the connection between religion and the fear of death, and describes mankind's ignorance of the cure for their fear. In the last paragraph (127–135) he summarizes the two main problems. If we would cease to fear the gods, we must learn the laws of natural science. If we would cease to fear death, we must learn the nature of the soul.

[This pattern of thought changed as Lucretius pro-
gressed with his work. Books I and II deal with the
nature of matter, that is, atoms. We should expect to
find, immediately after this, the subjects discussed in
Books V and VI, namely the formation of our "world",
astronomy, the origin of life, man's development, and
celestial and terrestrial phenomena such as thunder
and earthquakes. Meanwhile in Book III Lucretius
deals with the nature of the soul, gives proofs of its
mortality, and bursts forth into his magnificent tirade
against the folly of the fear of death. Book IV is concerned with the nature of sight, thought, hearing, etc.
More will be said later about Lucretius' arrangement
of his work.[1]]

I. I. 50–135

50 Quod superest, vacuas auris animumque sagacem
    semotum a curis adhibe veram ad rationem,
    ne mea dona tibi studio disposta fideli,
    intellecta prius quam sint, contempta relinquas.
    nam tibi de summa caeli ratione deumque
55 disserere incipiam et rerum primordia pandam,
    unde omnis natura creet res auctet alatque
    quove eadem rursum natura perempta resolvat,
    quae nos materiem et genitalia corpora rebus
    reddunda in ratione vocare et semina rerum
60 appellare suemus et haec eadem usurpare
    corpora prima, quod ex illis sunt omnia primis.
       Humana ante oculos foede cum vita iaceret
    in terris oppressa gravi sub religione
    quae caput a caeli regionibus ostendebat
65 horribili super aspectu mortalibus instans,
    primum Graius homo mortalis tollere contra
    est oculos ausus primusque obsistere contra,

---

[1] See Index, *s.v.* Structure of the *de R. N.*

quem neque fama deum nec fulmina nec minitanti
murmure compressit caelum, sed eo magis acrem
irritat animi virtutem, effringere ut arta   70
naturae primus portarum claustra cupiret.
ergo vivida vis animi pervicit, et extra
processit longe flammantia moenia mundi
atque omne immensum peragravit mente animoque,
unde refert nobis victor quid possit oriri,   75
quid nequeat, finita potestas denique cuique
quanam sit ratione atque alte terminus haerens.
quare religio pedibus subiecta vicissim
obteritur, nos exaequat victoria caelo.
    Illud in his rebus vereor, ne forte rearis   80
impia te rationis inire elementa viamque
indugredi sceleris. quod contra saepius illa
religio peperit scelerosa atque impia facta.
Aulide quo pacto Triviai virginis aram
Iphianassai turparunt sanguine foede   85
ductores Danaum delecti, prima virorum.
cui simul infula virgineos circumdata comptus
ex utraque pari malarum parte profusast,
et maestum simul ante aras adstare parentem
sensit et hunc propter ferrum celare ministros   90
aspectuque suo lacrimas effundere civis,
muta metu terram genibus summissa petebat.
nec miserae prodesse in tali tempore quibat
quod patrio princeps donarat nomine regem.
nam sublata virum manibus tremibundaque ad aras   95
deductast, non ut sollemni more sacrorum
perfecto posset claro comitari Hymenaeo,
sed casta inceste nubendi tempore in ipso
hostia concideret mactatu maesta parentis,
exitus ut classi felix faustusque daretur.   100
tantum religio potuit suadere malorum.

    Tutemet a nobis iam quovis tempore vatum
terriloquis victus dictis desciscere quaeres.
    quippe etenim quam multa tibi iam fingere possunt
105 somnia quae vitae rationes vertere possint
fortunasque tuas omnis turbare timore!
    et merito. nam si certam finem esse viderent
aerumnarum homines, aliqua ratione valerent
reiigionibus atque minis obsistere vatum.
110 nunc ratio nulla est restandi, nulla facultas,
aeternas quoniam poenas in morte timendumst.
    ignoratur enim quae sit natura animai,
nata sit an contra nascentibus insinuetur,
et simul intereat nobiscum morte dirempta
115 an tenebras Orci visat vastasque lacunas
an pecudes alias divinitus insinuet se,
Ennius ut noster cecinit qui primus amoeno
detulit ex Helicone perenni fronde coronam,
per gentis Italas hominum quae clara clueret;
120 etsi praeterea tamen esse Acherusia templa
Ennius aeternis exponit versibus edens,
quo neque permaneant animae neque corpora nostra,
sed quaedam simulacra modis pallentia miris;
unde sibi exortam semper florentis Homeri
125 commemorat speciem lacrimas effundere salsas
coepisse et rerum naturam expandere dictis.
    Quapropter bene cum superis de rebus habenda
nobis est ratio, solis lunaeque meatus
qua fiant ratione, et qua vi quaeque gerantur
130 in terris, tunc cum primis ratione sagaci
unde anima atque animi constet natura videndum,
et quae res nobis vigilantibus obvia mentis
terrificet morbo adfectis somnoque sepultis,
cernere uti videamur eos audireque coram,
135 morte obita quorum tellus amplectitur ossa.

In Passage 1 we have seen Lucretius' purpose unfolded. In the following passage he explains his choice
of medium; he explains, that is, why he has chosen to
put his message into *poetry*. He offers two different
explanations. First he speaks of *laudis spes magna* and
amor musarum—motives such as enter into the writing
of all poetry. Then, as if conscious that *amor musarum*
is a passion of which a true Epicurean could hardly
approve, he suggests a quite different explanation: in
a famous simile, he compares his poetry with the
honey that is smeared on the lip of the cup to persuade
a child to take his medicine. This second explanation
rings a little false when we consider the intensity of
feeling that inspires much of the *de R.N.* We may
justifiably conclude that his second explanation is a
mere rationalization of the natural impulse which drove
him, as other poets, to find an outlet for his intense
feelings in poetry.[1]

2. I. 921–950

Nunc age quod superest cognosce et clarius audi.　921
nec me animi fallit quam sint obscura; sed acri
percussit thyrso laudis spes magna meum cor
et simul incussit suavem mi in pectus amorem
musarum, quo nunc instinctus mente vigenti　925
avia Pieridum peragro loca nullius ante
trita solo. iuvat integros accedere fontis
atque haurire, iuvatque novos decerpere flores
insignemque meo capiti petere inde coronam
unde prius nulli velarint tempora musae;　930
primum quod magnis doceo de rebus et artis
religionum animum nodis exsolvere pergo,
deinde quod obscura de re tam lucida pango
carmina, musaeo contingens cuncta lepore.

[1] See Intro. (ii).

935 id quoque enim non ab nulla ratione videtur;
sed veluti pueris absinthia taetra medentes
cum dare conantur, prius oras pocula circum
contingunt mellis dulci flavoque liquore,
ut puerorum aetas improvida ludificetur
940 labrorum tenus, interea perpotet amarum
absinthi laticem deceptaque non capiatur,
sed potius tali pacto recreata valescat,
sic ego nunc, quoniam haec ratio plerumque videtur
tristior esse quibus non est tractata, retroque
945 vulgus abhorret ab hac, volui tibi suaviloquenti
carmine Pierio rationem exponere nostram
et quasi musaeo dulci contingere melle,
si tibi forte animum tali ratione tenere
versibus in nostris possem, dum perspicis omnem
950 naturam rerum qua constet compta figura.

EPICUREANISM

A. CANONIC,[1] THEORY OF KNOWLEDGE

Every system of philosophy which sets out to explain
the universe must be based on its answer to one fundamental question: What is *knowing*?

The trend which philosophy was taking immediately
before Epicurus is illustrated in the views of Pyrrho
the Sceptic (*c.* 365–275 B.C.) about this question.
Pyrrho maintained that there is no evidence to lead
us to trust the senses rather than reason or reason
rather than the senses. We cannot *know*: the best we
can do is to "suspend judgement".

On such a basis it was difficult to construct a philosophy capable of teaching men how to live. "How to

---

[1] So called by Epicurus, from κανών, "rule".

live" was the subject which concerned Epicurus most. He therefore answered the question, What is knowing? in the way in which the plain man unconsciously answers it, and threw overboard most of the apparatus of philosophic speculation on the subject. He declared quite simply that all true knowledge comes from the senses and that the senses are infallible. *The infallibility of the senses* is the basis of the whole Epicurean system, the first principle of Epicurus' "Canonic".

Lucretius assumes this principle throughout the *de R.N.*, but he does not give a full statement of it till the middle of the fourth book. He is there discussing the nature of sight, a subject which naturally leads on to the question, How can optical illusions be explained if the senses are infallible?

He gives us a whole picture-gallery of scenes in each of which the observer is liable to be the victim of an optical illusion, and asserts that in each instance it is not the eyes that are at fault, but the mind or reason, which has drawn false inferences from the evidence supplied to it by the eyes. He then attacks the Sceptics. If we deny the possibility of knowledge, how can we know even that we do not know? Before we presume to attack the senses we must find something truer than they. Reason will not do, for reason is based wholly on the evidence supplied by the senses. The senses are the only guides we have: it is the senses that prevent us from falling over cliffs and the like; and if we doubt the senses we cut at the root not merely of reason but of life itself.

[Whatever we may think of the philosophical value of this first principle, we cannot overestimate its value as the seed of much of Lucretius' poetry. "The trust in the senses is the ultimate cause of those many illustrations from common experience, which are so largely responsible for the beauty and the poetic wealth

of the whole poem.'[1] Poetry cannot lose touch with
sensuous experience without running the risk of ceasing
to be poetry. Epicureanism thus possessed a great
advantage over other systems of philosophy (at least
over the other systems of philosophy in vogue in
Lucretius' day) as a theme for a poet. The following
passage is a good example of Lucretius' use of "illustrations from common experience".]

3. IV. 379–521

379   Nec tamen hic oculos falli concedimus hilum.
nam quocumque loco sit lux atque umbra tueri
illorum est; eadem vero sint lumina necne,
umbraque quae fuit hic eadem nunc transeat illuc,
an potius fiat paulo quod diximus ante,
hoc animi demum ratio discernere debet,
385 nec possunt oculi naturam noscere rerum.
proinde animi vitium hoc oculis adfingere noli.
qua vehimur navi, fertur, cum stare videtur;
quae manet in statione, ea praeter creditur ire.
et fugere ad puppim colles campique videntur
390 quos agimus praeter navem velisque volamus.
sidera cessare aetheriis adfixa cavernis
cuncta videntur, et assiduo sunt omnia motu,
quandoquidem longos obitus exorta revisunt,
cum permensa suo sunt caelum corpore claro.
395 solque pari ratione manere et luna videntur
in statione, ea quae ferri res indicat ipsa.
exstantesque procul medio de gurgite montes
classibus inter quos liber patet exitus ingens,
insula coniunctis tamen ex his una videtur.
400 atria versari et circumcursare columnae
usque adeo fit uti pueris videantur, ubi ipsi

---

[1] B. tr. p. 14.

desierunt verti, vix ut iam credere possint
non supra sese ruere omnia tecta minari.
iamque rubrum tremulis iubar ignibus erigere alte
cum coeptat natura supraque extollere montis,   405
quos tibi tum supra sol montis esse videtur
comminus ipse suo contingens fervidus igni,
vix absunt nobis missus bis mille sagittae,
vix etiam cursus quingentos saepe veruti.
inter eos solemque iacent immania ponti   410
aequora substrata aetheriis ingentibus oris,
interiectaque sunt terrarum milia multa
quae variae retinent gentes et saecla ferarum.
at collectus aquae digitum non altior unum,
qui lapides inter sistit per strata viarum,   415
despectum praebet sub terras impete tanto,
a terris quantum caeli patet altus hiatus;
nubila despicere et caelum ut videare videre et
corpora mirando sub terras abdita caelo.
denique ubi in medio nobis equus acer obhaesit   420
flumine et in rapidas amnis despeximus undas,
stantis equi corpus transversum ferre videtur
vis et in adversum flumen contrudere raptim,
et quocumque oculos traiecimus omnia ferri
et fluere assimili nobis ratione videntur.   425
porticus aequali quamvis est denique ductu
stansque in perpetuum paribus suffulta columnis,
longa tamen parte ab summa cum tota videtur,
paulatim trahit angusti fastigia coni,
tecta solo iungens atque omnia dextera laevis   430
donec in obscurum coni conduxit acumen.
in pelago nautis ex undis ortus in undis
sol fit uti videatur obire et condere lumen;
quippe ubi nil aliud nisi aquam caelumque tuentur;
ne leviter credas labefactari undique sensus.   435

at maris ignaris in portu clauda videntur
navigia aplustris fractis obnitier undae.
nam quaecumque supra rorem salis edita pars est
remorum, recta est, et recta superne guberna.
440 quae demersa liquorem obeunt, refracta videntur
omnia converti sursumque supina reverti
et reflexa prope in summo fluitare liquore.
raraque per caelum cum venti nubila portant
tempore nocturno, tum splendida signa videntur
445 labier adversum nimbos atque ire superne
longe aliam in partem ac vera ratione feruntur.
at si forte oculo manus uni subdita subter
pressit eum, quodam sensu fit uti videantur
omnia quae tuimur fieri tum bina tuendo,
450 bina lucernarum florentia lumina flammis
binaque per totas aedes geminare supellex
et duplices hominum facies et corpora bina.
denique cum suavi devinxit membra sopore
somnus et in summa corpus iacet omne quiete,
455 tum vigilare tamen nobis et membra movere
nostra videmur, et in noctis caligine caeca
cernere censemus solem lumenque diurnum,
conclusoque loco caelum mare flumina montis
mutare et campos pedibus transire videmur,
460 et sonitus audire, severa silentia noctis
undique cum constent, et reddere dicta tacentes.
cetera de genere hoc mirande multa videmus,
quae violare fidem quasi sensibus omnia quaerunt,
nequiquam, quoniam pars horum maxima fallit
465 propter opinatus animi quos addimus ipsi,
pro visis ut sint quae non sunt sensibu' visa.
nam nil aegrius est quam res secernere apertas
ab dubiis, animus quas ab se protinus addit.
    Denique nil sciri siquis putat, id quoque nescit

an sciri possit, quoniam nil scire fatetur.   470
hunc igitur contra mittam contendere causam,
qui capite ipse sua in statuit vestigia sese.
et tamen hoc quoque uti concedam scire, at id ipsum
quaeram, cum in rebus veri nil viderit ante,
unde sciat quid sit scire et nescire vicissim,   475
notitiam veri quae res falsique crearit
et dubium certo quae res differre probarit.
invenies primis ab sensibus esse creatam
notitiem veri neque sensus posse refelli.
nam maiore fide debet reperirier illud,   480
sponte sua veris quod possit vincere falsa.
quid maiore fide porro quam sensus haberi
debet? an ab sensu falso ratio orta valebit
dicere eos contra, quae tota ab sensibus orta est?
qui nisi sunt veri, ratio quoque falsa fit omnis.   485
an poterunt oculos aures reprehendere, an auris
tactus? an hunc porro tactum sapor arguet oris,
an confutabunt nares oculive revincent?
non, ut opinor, ita est. nam sorsum cuique potestas
divisast, sua vis cuiquest, ideoque necesse est   490
et quod molle sit et gelidum fervensve seorsum
et sorsum varios rerum sentire colores
et quaecumque coloribu' sint coniuncta videre.
sorsus item sapor oris habet vim, sorsus odores
nascuntur, sorsum sonitus. ideoque necesse est   495
non possint alios alii convincere sensus.
nec porro poterunt ipsi reprehendere sese,
aequa fides quoniam debebit semper haberi.
proinde quod in quoquest his visum tempore, verumst.
        Et si non poterit ratio dissolvere causam,   500
cur ea quae fuerint iuxtim quadrata, procul sint
visa rotunda, tamen praestat rationis egentem
reddere mendose causas utriusque figurae,

quam manibus manifesta suis emittere quoquam
505 et violare fidem primam et convellere tota
fundamenta quibus nixatur vita salusque.
non modo enim ratio ruat omnis, vita quoque ipsa
concidat extemplo, nisi credere sensibus ausis
praecipitesque locos vitare et cetera quae sint
510 in genere hoc fugienda, sequi contraria quae sint.
illa tibi est igitur verborum copia cassa
omnis quae contra sensus instructa paratast.
denique ut in fabrica, si pravast regula prima,
normaque si fallax rectis regionibus exit,
515 et libella aliqua si ex parti claudicat hilum,
omnia mendose fieri atque obstipa necesse est
prava cubantia prona supina atque absona tecta,
iam ruere ut quaedam videantur velle, ruantque
prodita iudiciis fallacibus omnia primis,
520 sic igitur ratio tibi rerum prava necessest
falsaque sit, falsis quaecumque ab sensibus ortast.

This first principle is of course beset with difficulties
How can the senses give us knowledge of things outside
direct sense-perception? How, for instance, can the
senses of themselves build up a philosophic system
such as Epicureanism?

Epicurus, being interested chiefly in the practical or
ethical side of philosophy, did not attempt to probe
very deeply into the difficulties of his fundamental
principle. But he does attempt to explain *how "concepts" are formed in the mind*, which brings us to the
second general principle of his Canonic.

[The summary that follows is based on the scattered
passages where Lucretius touches on the subject in
passing. The special difficulties raised by Epicurus'
more ample treatment will not be discussed.]

The formation of mental concepts is closely analogous to the process of physical seeing. Physical sight, according to Epicurus, is caused by the "Idols" (*simulacra*, εἴδωλα) which are continually being cast off by every object. The Idol of an object is composed of the outer layer of atoms, each layer being of an inconceivable fineness. Lucretius' simile (IV. 58) is helpful: "as when the grasshoppers lay aside their smooth coats in summer". The atoms of the Idol, which moves with astonishing speed, impinge upon the atoms of our eyes and so cause sight.[1]

A mental concept is always regarded as a "visualization" of this or that. The simplest type of concept is the result of a series of ordinary sense-perceptions. For instance, having observed many individual horses, we have the general concept "horse". Or again, having observed on many occasions that fire is hot, we *know*, as a general concept, that all fire is hot. This or any other such concept remains true until such time as the senses may give us reason to revise it. "Concept" in Lucretius is *notitia* or *notities*, in Epicurus πρόληψις (the Greek word implies that we have an anticipation of what we shall find to be the case if given circumstances recur in the future. I shall burn my finger if I put it in the fire).

But how, we may ask, can concepts be formed in the mind of things of which it has never had direct sense-perception, e.g. the concept of an atom? The answer is that the mind has the power of "projecting itself" upon the infinite store of Idols, whether outside or stored up in the mind, and of selecting from them and of forming combinations between them, which may result in the creation of a new concept. This will be a kind of composite photograph in the mind. An example given by Lucretius is as follows: The atoms have no

---

[1] More fully described under B (d).

colour, but yet have shape. We can never have direct sense-perception of anything that has shape but no colour. But consider the blind: they know "shape" by touch, although for them it is never linked with colour. Thus by a "projection of the mind" we may "visualize", that is, conceive of, colourless forms (II. 730 ff.). Projection of the mind = *animi iniectus* = ἐπιβολὴ τῆς διανοίας.[1]

This theory of knowledge is open to many criticisms,[2] of which it will be enough to mention one or two. For instance, there is the kind of criticism which Plutarch makes. The bath feels hot to you, cold to me: but all sensations are true: the reality then of quality in the object disappears. We are left with purely subjective standards of judgement: the individual man is "the measure of all things". This is not far removed from the Scepticism which Epicurus set out to avoid. Again, Epicurus makes no attempt to explain how continuity of consciousness can exist amid the constant flux of atoms. What is the ultimate cause of the mind's "projecting" itself? Again, the "Idol" theory of mental visualization is crude and childish, as is the theory of physical sight to which it corresponds. In short, we must recognize that Epicurus' theory of knowledge is an exceptionally unsatisfactory foundation for a system of philosophy.

But as a foundation for physical science it served its

[1] For an explanation of the process of "projection" see IV. 722 ff., esp. 777 ff. For the term see II. 740 (*animi iniectus*), II. 1047 (*animi iactus*), and perhaps II. 1080. For *notitia* see II. 124, 745, IV. 476, V. 124, 182, 1047.

[2] As are all theories of knowledge, it is hardly necessary to add. All we can say is that some are less unsatisfactory than others. Epicurus, having a house to build, chose to found it on sand rather than to spend time looking for a rock which did not exist. We have reason to be glad of his choice, which gave us the *de R.N.*

purpose. "Lucretius has always enjoyed the esteem of
men of science because...he insisted that the evidence
of the senses was the only means at our disposal for
gaining knowledge of the external world. He set out
to create a science free from mysticism, and, however
desirable mysticism may be in other human activities,
experience has proved that mechanism is a much more
powerful weapon for scientific investigation—naturally,
since science deals with the mechanical aspect of nature
only."[1] The evidence of the senses leads to the pro-
visional concept, which is valid until modified by
further evidence of the senses. This, the method of
Epicurus, is nothing less than the inductive method,
which is essential in the acquisition of scientific knowledge.

This brings us to a third point in Epicurean Canonic,
which may be summarized as follows.

The evidence on which scientific enquiry must be
based is supplied by the senses. Sometimes the senses
will give direct evidence that such and such is so: often
we have to be content with an explanation in whose
favour there is no stronger argument than that it is not
contradicted by the evidence of the senses. In such
cases there are usually several possible explanations: to
the Epicurean all remain equally true until such time
as the senses give direct evidence in support of one
or against another. For instance, the Nile floods every
summer. Why? Lucretius gives us four alternative
explanations.

*4. VI. 703–737

Sunt aliquot quoque res quarum unam dicere causam 703
non satis est, verum pluris, unde una tamen sit;

---

[1] Andrade, p. xix.

corpus ut exanimum siquod procul ipse iacere
conspicias hominis, fit ut omnis dicere causas
conveniat leti, dicatur ut illius una.
nam neque eum ferro nec frigore vincere possis
interiisse neque a morbo neque forte veneno,
710 verum aliquid genere esse ex hoc quod contigit ei
scimus. item in multis hoc rebus dicere habemus.
　　Nilus in aestatem crescit campisque redundat
unicus in terris Aegypti totius amnis.
is rigat Aegyptum medium per saepe calorem,
715 aut quia sunt aestate aquilones ostia contra,
anni tempore eo qui etesiae esse feruntur,
et contra fluvium flantes remorantur et undas
cogentes sursus replent coguntque manere.
nam dubio procul haec adverso flabra feruntur
720 flumine, quae gelidis ab stellis axis aguntur.
ille ex aestifera parti venit amnis ab austro,
inter nigra virum percocto saecla colore
exoriens penitus media ab regione diei.
est quoque uti possit magnus congestus harenae
725 fluctibus adversis oppilare ostia contra,
cum mare permotum ventis ruit intus harenam;
quo fit uti pacto liber minus exitus amnis
et proclivis item fiat minus impetus undis.
fit quoque uti pluviae forsan magis ad caput ei
730 tempore eo fiant, quod etesia flabra aquilonum
nubila coniciunt in eas tunc omnia partis.
scilicet ad mediam regionem eiecta diei
cum convenerunt, ibi ad altos denique montis
contrusae nubes coguntur vique premuntur.
735 forsitan Aethiopum penitus de montibus altis
crescat, ubi in campos albas descendere ningues
tabificis subigit radiis sol omnia lustrans.

This is admirable as far as it goes. Observation of the phenomena leads to the formation of alternative possible theories. Final judgement is suspended until further evidence is forthcoming.

The next step in the pursuit of scientific knowledge is the discovery of further evidence by more detailed observation and, where possible, by experimentation. This next step Epicurus and his followers signally failed to take. So long as *some* mechanical explanation not inconsistent with the evidence of the senses could be found, so long as the supernatural was altogether excluded, Epicurus was content. It did not matter whether a particular explanation was correct or not, provided that the senses did not show it to be impossible. No Epicurean would have thought it worth while to visit Egypt in order to observe the effect of the etesian winds or of the sand-bar. Lucretius only once mentions an experiment—if it can be so called (VI. 1044 ff.). "I have seen...filings of iron rave within brass basins, when this Magnet stone had been placed under." There was no advance in Epicurean "science" between the time of Epicurus and the time of Lucretius, and it is doubtful whether Lucretius himself adds anything to the body of scientific theory compiled by his master.

Natural Science is only of importance to the Epicurean as a prop to Ethics, because a knowledge of it rids men of fear of the supernatural. One explanation is as good as another provided it performs this function. Thus Epicurean science never advanced very far. But it embodied a number of bold and brilliant guesses and a grand if inadequately subtle conception of the nature of the universe.

B. RERUM NATURA, NATURAL SCIENCE

[Having dealt with the foundation of Epicurus' philosophy, we can now pass on to the subject of Lucretius' poem, Natural Science. In this section Lucretius himself will be our guide. By following the lines of his exposition we shall be able to gain an understanding of the structure both of Epicurean Natural Science and of Lucretius' poem. Thus the present section is intended to be a ground-plan of the whole of the *de R.N.*, consisting partly of selected passages from the original, partly of a summary of the intervening passages and a running commentary.

There is one class of exceptions to this general scheme, namely the prooemium at the beginning of each of the six books. The prooemium in Lucretius usually has no direct connection with what follows it, and for the sake of convenience a few general remarks about the prooemia will be made here instead of at the places where they occur. There are two main themes running through the prooemia: (1) praise of Epicurus (prooemia to Books I, III, V, VI), (2) the blessing conferred by a study of Epicurus' philosophy, namely, freedom from human fears and passions (Books I, II, III, VI). There are two passages which contain matter that is foreign to these main themes: (1) The prooemium to Book IV (ll. 1–25), which describes Lucretius' mission and method and is almost identical with ll. 926–950 of Book I (Passage 2 above). (2) The opening lines of Book I (ll. 1–43), which consist of an invocation to Venus. It is strange that Lucretius should begin his poem with a passage that appears at first sight to be inconsistent with his belief about the nature of the gods.[1] Various explanations are possible: Lucretius

[1] See B (g), pp. 78–83.

may merely be following poetical tradition in beginning his poem with an invocation to a deity; he may have wished thus to pay a compliment to Memmius, since (as we know from coins) Venus was the patron goddess of the Memmian gens; he may, with a suggestion of pantheism which often comes to the surface in the course of the *de R.N.*, have introduced Venus as a personification of the Life Force in nature. Whatever may have been the considerations present in Lucretius' mind, the result is a passage of great beauty.]

As the foundation of his system of Natural Science Epicurus took over, with some alterations, the atomic theory of Leucippus and Democritus. There were other theories which he might have chosen, but in choosing the atomic theory he was guided, as in all other parts of his system of philosophy, by the primary law of Canonic, namely that the senses are infallible. Of all the theories put forward by previous philosophers to explain the physical constitution of the universe,[1] the atomic theory alone was not contradicted by the evidence of the senses.

B (a) *Atoms and void.* Book I

I. 146–264. The first two principles enunciated by Lucretius correspond roughly to the doctrine now known as the conservation of matter. First, nothing can be created out of nothing. Second, nothing can be dissolved into nothing; things can be dissolved only into the first-bodies of matter, i.e. atoms. The universe is birthless, deathless, immutable.

I. 265–482. Next, the universe consists of matter and space: there is no third to these two. All things else

[1] For examples see I. 635–920.

are either "properties" (*coniuncta*) or "accidents"
(*eventa*) of matter and space. Lucretius explains this
in the following passage.

5. i. 418–482

418 Sed nunc ut repetam coeptum pertexere dictis,
omnis, ut est igitur per se, natura duabus
constitit in rebus; nam corpora sunt et inane,
haec in quo sita sunt et qua diversa moventur.
corpus enim per se communis dedicat esse
sensus; cui nisi prima fides fundata valebit,
haud erit occultis de rebus quo referentes
425 confirmare animi quicquam ratione queamus.
tum porro locus ac spatium, quod inane vocamus,
si nullum foret, haud usquam sita corpora possent
esse neque omnino quoquam diversa meare;
id quod iam supera tibi paulo ostendimus ante.
430 praeterea nil est quod possis dicere ab omni
corpore seiunctum secretumque esse ab inani,
quod quasi tertia sit numero natura reperta.
nam quodcumque erit, esse aliquid debebit id ipsum;
cui si tactus erit quamvis levis exiguusque,
435 augmine vel grandi vel parvo denique, dum sit,
corporis augebit numerum summamque sequetur.
sin intactile erit, nulla de parte quod ullam
rem prohibere queat per se transire meantem,
scilicet hoc id erit, vacuum quod inane vocamus.
440 praeterea per se quodcumque erit, aut faciet quid
aut aliis fungi debebit agentibus ipsum
aut erit ut possint in eo res esse gerique.
at facere et fungi sine corpore nulla potest res
nec praebere locum porro nisi inane vacansque.
445 ergo praeter inane et corpora tertia per se
nulla potest rerum in numero natura relinqui,

nec quae sub sensus cadat ullo tempore nostros
nec ratione animi quam quisquam possit apisci.
    Nam quaecumque cluent, aut his coniuncta duabus
rebus ea invenies aut horum eventa videbis.   450
coniunctum est id quod nusquam sine permitiali
discidio potis est seiungi seque gregari,
pondus uti saxis, calor ignist, liquor aquai,
tactus corporibus cunctis, intactus inani.
servitium contra paupertas divitiaeque,   455
libertas bellum concordia, cetera quorum
adventu manet incolumis natura abituque,
haec soliti sumus, ut par est, eventa vocare.
tempus item per se non est, sed rebus ab ipsis
consequitur sensus, transactum quid sit in aevo,   460
tum quae res instet, quid porro deinde sequatur.
nec per se quemquam tempus sentire fatendumst
semotum ab rerum motu placidaque quiete.
denique Tyndaridem raptam belloque subactas
Troiugenas gentis cum dicunt esse, videndumst   465
ne forte haec per se cogant nos esse fateri,
quando ea saecla hominum, quorum haec eventa fuerunt,
irrevocabilis abstulerit iam praeterita aetas.
namque aliud terris, aliud regionibus ipsis
eventum dici poterit quodcumque erit actum.   470
denique materies si rerum nulla fuisset
nec locus ac spatium, res in quo quaeque geruntur,
numquam Tyndaridis forma conflatus amoris
ignis, Alexandri Phrygio sub pectore gliscens,
clara accendisset saevi certamina belli,   475
nec clam durateus Troianis Pergama partu
inflammasset equus nocturno Graiugenarum;
perspicere ut possis res gestas funditus omnis
non ita uti corpus per se co   re neque esse,
nec ratione cluere eadem qua constet inane,   480

sed magis ut merito possis eventa vocare
corporis atque loci, res in quo quaeque gerantur.

There are three points arising out of Lucretius'
account of *coniuncta* and *eventa* which require some
comment.

First, if past events are but the "accidents" of the
material objects (= persons and things) and void which
played a necessary part in bringing them about, how
do such events become part of our consciousness in the
present, when those material objects are no more? The
answer may be that past events become "accidents" of
the minds of all who hear or read about them: they are
handed down as "accidents" of each of an unbroken
series of minds. How communication between one
mind and another is effected, is an awkward question,
which, so far as we know, Epicurus evaded.

Second, Time. Time, according to Epicurus, is
something that cannot be experienced or conceived of
except in relation to persons and things. Moreover, it
is not directly connected with persons and things, but
rather with the "actions" of persons and things (whether
they act or are acted upon). But the actions of persons
and things are but their "accidents": Time, therefore,
said Epicurus, is "an accident of accidents". (Since
we can conceive of no action outside Time, we might
have expected him to say rather "a property of accidents".) The problem of Time is one of those with
which the ancient world made little headway; and
though Epicurus does not probe into it very deeply,
his solution is adequate as a part of the system of philosophy intended for the man in the street.

Third, we must not understand from Lucretius'
account that *coniuncta* and *eventa* are in his opinion
two rigidly divided categories, so that we could say of
any quality "This is a 'property'" or "This is an
'accident'". There is no rigid division: we can only

distinguish which qualities are "properties" and which "accidents" if we judge them in relation to specific things. Heat, says Lucretius, is a "property" of fire. But it is an "accident" of coffee: my coffee is still coffee even though it be cold. Wealth, says Lucretius, is normally an "accident". But it can be a "property": remove a rich man's wealth and he is no longer "a rich man" but something else. We must therefore remember that the terms *coniuncta* and *eventa* are flexible, and that the examples given by Lucretius are only given for the sake of example and not as definitions which cover every instance.

The following is a summary of the account of things so far given by Lucretius. "Having thus enunciated his doctrine of 'properties' and 'accidents' Lucretius has from the Atomic point of view covered the whole field of possible existence. All things which can be the objects of perception or of thought must be either one of the two ultimate realities, atoms and space, or concrete bodies, formed by their combination, or the 'properties' or 'accidents' of these, or, in the single instance of Time, an 'accident of accidents'."[1]

i. 483–920. Lucretius returns to the *primordia*.[2] He shows first that they are entirely solid, unlike all other bodies, e.g. iron, which are composed of atoms *and* void; second, that they are indivisible and therefore eternal. Other theories of the ultimate constitution of things are untrue, because they are refuted by the evidence of the senses. Lucretius demonstrates the

---

[1] Quoted with minor alterations from B., p. 309.
[2] It is perhaps well to state at the outset that the Epicurean atom, though it may be the historical ancestor of the conception of the atom held by modern physicists, bears but little resemblance to its complex descendant.

falsity of three such theories, those of Heraclitus,
Empedocles, and Anaxagoras.

   I. 951–1117. The last part of the first book is concerned with the question, Are the two constituents of
the sum of things (matter and void) boundless in
extent? Lucretius in the following passage appeals to
the evidence of the senses with a fine imaginative
picture in support of the view that the universe is
boundless.

6. I. 951–983

951   Sed quoniam docui solidissima materiai
   corpora perpetuo volitare invicta per aevum,
   nunc age, summai quaedam sit finis eorum
   necne sit, evolvamus; item quod inane repertumst
955 seu locus ac spatium, res in quo quaeque gerantur,
   pervideamus utrum finitum funditus omne
   constet an immensum pateat vasteque profundum.
     Omne quod est igitur nulla regione viarum
   finitumst; namque extremum debebat habere.
960 extremum porro nullius posse videtur
   esse, nisi ultra sit quod finiat; ut videatur
   quo non longius haec sensus natura sequatur.
   nunc extra summam quoniam nil esse fatendum,
   non habet extremum, caret ergo fine modoque.
965 nec refert quibus adsistas regionibus eius;
   usque adeo, quem quisque locum possedit, in omnis
   tantundem partis infinitum omne relinquit.
   praeterea si iam finitum constituatur
   omne quod est spatium, siquis procurrat ad oras
970 ultimus extremas iaciatque volatile telum,
   id validis utrum contortum viribus ire
   quo fuerit missum mavis longeque volare,
   an prohibere aliquid censes obstareque posse?

alterutrum fatearis enim sumasque necessest.
quorum utrumque tibi effugium praecludit et omne   975
cogit ut exempta concedas fine patere.
nam sive est aliquid quod probeat efficiatque
quominu' quo missum est veniat finique locet se,
sive foras fertur, non est a fine profectum.
hoc pacto sequar atque, oras ubicumque locaris   980
extremas, quaeram quid telo denique fiat.
fiet uti nusquam possit consistere finis
effugiumque fugae prolatet copia semper.

Nowadays, when light-rays are curved and the universe is spoken of as "finite but unbounded",[1] a
scientist might reply to Lucretius that the spear will
indeed fly forward, but that it will travel *in a curve*,
and might ultimately, were its velocity unimpaired,
strike the spearsman in the back.

Lucretius proceeds to split the question into two and
shows both (1) that space is infinite (in extent), and
(2) that the atoms are infinite (in number). With this
the first book closes.

B (b) *The formation of things out of*
atoms and void. Book II

In his second book Lucretius discusses first the motion
of the atoms, which is responsible both for the formation and for the dissolution of things.

II. 62-332. Atoms are ever in motion. Two causes
of their motion are: (1) their weight, which causes
them to move ceaselessly downwards in space;[2] (2) the

[1] As an analogy in two dimensions: the *surface* of a
sphere is finite but unbounded.
[2] We here of course come up against a difficulty, of which
Epicurus himself was conscious. In an infinite universe

blows which they strike one upon another, impinging and rebounding in all directions. (There is a third cause of their motion which we come to in a moment.) They are equally in motion whether they be free atoms moving in space or atoms united to form things. They move at astonishing velocity, surpassing the velocity of light.

In the following passage Lucretius discusses the third cause of their motion, which has an important bearing on his ethical as well as on his scientific theory. This third cause is the atomic swerve.

The primary cause of the motion of the atoms is their weight, which carries them downwards through space. How then do those collisions come about which start motion in other directions and so enable atoms to combine?

Some might suppose that heavier atoms fall more swiftly than lighter atoms and so set up collisions. With remarkable acuteness Epicurus had rejected this theory. Although we see that heavier bodies fall more swiftly than lighter bodies through air[1], in the void there is no air-resistance and therefore all the atoms must fall at equal speed, whatever their weight.

There is nothing for it therefore but to postulate that the atoms have the power of making an infinitesimal swerve from their straight downward course. Once this is admitted the atoms are able to impinge upon one another and the whole system of blows and rebounds naturally follows. It thus becomes possible for the atoms to combine to form things.

But the theory of the atomic swerve does more than

"downwards", "upwards", etc. have no meaning. But on this earth all things appear to the senses to fall downwards when possible; and Epicurus was thus led to draw a false analogy.

[1] Too simple a statement, as Galileo showed.

account for the formation of things. If there were no
atomic swerve and every movement of the atoms could
be explained on purely mechanical lines, as being
necessitated by the movements that have gone before,
whence comes *the power of free-will, which our senses
tell us we possess*? Since the mind is but a collection
of atoms, each separate atom must have a power corresponding to the power of free-will possessed by the
group of atoms which together form the mind. Free-
will *is*, in a literal and material sense, the swerve of
the atoms.[1]

7. II. 216–293

Illud in his quoque te rebus cognoscere avemus,   216
corpora cum deorsum rectum per inane feruntur
ponderibus propriis, incerto tempore ferme
incertisque locis spatio depellere paulum,
tantum quod momen mutatum dicere possis.   220
quod nisi declinare solerent, omnia deorsum,
imbris uti guttae, caderent per inane profundum,
nec foret offensus natus nec plaga creata
principiis: ita nil umquam natura creasset.

Quod si forte aliquis credit graviora potesse   225
corpora, quo citius rectum per inane feruntur,
incidere ex supero levioribus atque ita plagas
gignere quae possint genitalis reddere motus,
avius a vera longe ratione recedit.
nam per aquas quaecumque cadunt atque aera rarum, 230
haec pro ponderibus casus celerare necessest
propterea quia corpus aquae naturaque tenvis
aeris haud possunt aeque rem quamque morari,

---

[1] The individual atom is not of course conceived of as
possessing conscious volition which produces the swerve:
it should rather be described as having "a mechanical freedom corresponding to the psychical freedom of the will"
(B. p. 323).

sed citius cedunt gravioribus exsuperata.
235 at contra nulli de nulla parte neque ullo
tempore inane potest vacuum subsistere rei,
quin, sua quod natura petit, concedere pergat;
omnia quapropter debent per inane quietum
aeque ponderibus non aequis concita ferri.
240 haud igitur poterunt levioribus incidere umquam
ex supero graviora neque ictus gignere per se
qui varient motus per quos natura gerat res.
quare etiam atque etiam paulum inclinare necessest
corpora; nec plus quam minimum, ne fingere motus
245 obliquos videamur et id res vera refutet.
namque hoc in promptu manifestumque esse videmus,
pondera, quantum in sest, non posse obliqua meare,
ex supero cum praecipitant, quod cernere possis.
sed nil omnino recta regione viai
250 declinare quis est qui †possit cernere sese?†
Denique si semper motus conectitur omnis
et vetere exoritur semper novus ordine certo
nec declinando faciunt primordia motus
principium quoddam quod fati foedera rumpat,
255 ex infinito ne causam causa sequatur,
libera per terras unde haec animantibus exstat,
unde est haec, inquam, fatis avulsa voluntas
per quam progredimur quo ducit quemque voluptas,
declinamus item motus nec tempore certo
260 nec regione loci certa, sed ubi ipsa tulit mens?
nam dubio procul his rebus sua cuique voluntas
principium dat et hinc motus per membra rigantur.
nonne vides etiam patefactis tempore puncto
carceribus non posse tamen prorumpere equorum
265 vim cupidam tam de subito quam mens avet ipsa?
omnis enim totum per corpus materiai
copia conciri debet, concita per artus

omnis ut studium mentis conixa sequatur;
ut videas initum motus a corde creari
ex animique voluntate id procedere primum,   270
inde dari porro per totum corpus et artus.
nec similest ut cum impulsi procedimus ictu
viribus alterius magnis magnoque coactu.
nam tum materiem totius corporis omnem
perspicuumst nobis invitis ire rapique,   275
donec eam refrenavit per membra voluntas.
iamne vides igitur, quamquam vis extera multos
pellat et invitos cogat procedere saepe
praecipitesque rapi, tamen esse in pectore nostro
quiddam quod contra pugnare obstareque possit?   280
cuius ad arbitrium quoque copia materiai
cogitur interdum flecti per membra per artus
et proiecta refrenatur retroque residit.
quare in seminibus quoque idem fateare necessest,
esse aliam praeter plagas et pondera causam   285
motibus, unde haec est nobis innata potestas,
de nilo quoniam fieri nil posse videmus.
pondus enim prohibet ne plagis omnia fiant
externa quasi vi. sed ne mens ipsa necessum
intestinum habeat cunctis in rebus agendis   290
et devicta quasi cogatur ferre patique,
id facit exiguum clinamen principiorum
nec regione loci certa nec tempore certo.

Res ficta pueriliter says Cicero of the theory of the
atomic swerve, and so have most critics thought from
Epicurus' day to this. Epicurus has made an obvious
breach in his own first principle, that "nothing can be
created out of nothing": for the swerve has no material
cause whatever. There can be no doubt about his inconsistency, but we should ask ourselves a question put
by Munro, "What system-monger but somewhere or

other reaches a point where reason must be silent or self-contradictory?" The facts that atoms collide and that man has free-will must somehow be accounted for.

There was also a practical moral reason which must have weighed with a man of Epicurus' interests.[1] His chief purpose was always to combat the beliefs of orthodox religion. But he saw that there was a yet greater foe to the good life. "It were better", he wrote, "to follow the myths about the gods than to become a slave to the 'destiny' of the natural philosophers: for the former suggests a hope of placating the gods by worship, whereas the latter involves a necessity which knows no placation."[2] The only *logical* conclusion to be drawn from an entirely materialist system, such as that of Epicurus, is that everything in our lives is determined for us by necessity: never at any point have we freedom of choice, and therefore it is useless to try to construct a system of morals. Epicurus, being primarily interested in morals, preferred to sacrifice the consistency of his physical system rather than to admit the impossibility of moral choice.

The theory of the atomic swerve—*exiguum clinamen* —both accounts for the formation of all things in the universe, and stands as the fundamental principle upholding human liberty. As Munro said, "there is something grand and poetical in its very simplicity". It is a principle which unifies the whole universe and annuls the dividing line between what we call living and lifeless matter. In this it is not only poetic but perhaps after all not un-scientific: for there is reason to suppose that the dividing line between living and lifeless matter will not indefinitely resist the assault of modern experimental chemistry. J. S. Huxley writes

[1] The doctrine of the atomic swerve is Epicurus' chief departure from the atomic theory of Democritus.
[2] B. Epic. *Ep.* III. 134.

(1923), "we must...believe that not only living matter, but all matter, is associated with something of the same general description as mind in higher animals", and he argues that a new word is wanted to describe the "world-stuff" which is both matter and mind.[1] S. Francis hit the nail on the head when he spoke of Brother Sun and Sister Moon.

Having dealt with the motion of the atoms Lucretius goes on next to discuss the shapes of the atoms.

II. 333-477. Amongst the atoms there are differences both of size and of shape. We see an analogy to this in the differences which exist between all individual creatures or objects, even when they belong to the same species. Moreover, these differences in things *can* only be explained if we assume that there are also differences amongst the atoms: otherwise nothing could differ from anything else. To the differences amongst the atoms must be attributed all the differences of sensation, e.g. the difference between a smooth, sweet taste, and a harsh, bitter taste.

*8. II. 333-407

Nunc age iam deinceps cunctarum exordia rerum   333
qualia sint et quam longe distantia formis
percipe, multigenis quam sint variata figuris;
non quo multa parum simili sint praedita forma,
sed quia non vulgo paria omnibus omnia constant.
nec mirum; nam cum sit eorum copia tanta
ut neque finis, uti docui, neque summa sit ulla,
debent nimirum non omnibus omnia prorsum   340
esse pari filo similique adfecta figura.
praeterea genus humanum mutaeque natantes
squamigerum pecudes et laeta armenta feraeque

---

[1] *Essays of a Biologist*, quoted by B. p. 322.

et variae volucres, laetantia quae loca aquarum
345 concelebrant circum ripas fontisque lacusque,
et quae pervulgant nemora avia pervolitantes;
quorum unum quidvis generatim sumere perge,
invenies tamen inter se differre figuris.
nec ratione alia proles cognoscere matrem
350 nec mater posset prolem; quod posse videmus
nec minus atque homines inter se nota cluere.
nam saepe ante deum vitulus delubra decora
turicremas propter mactatus concidit aras
sanguinis exspirans calidum de pectore flumen.
355 at mater viridis saltus orbata peragrans
† non quit † humi pedibus vestigia pressa bisulcis,
omnia convisens oculis loca si queat usquam
conspicere amissum fetum, completque querelis
frondiferum nemus adsistens et crebra revisit
360 ad stabulum desiderio perfixa iuvenci,
nec tenerae salices atque herbae rore vigentes
fluminaque illa queunt summis labentia ripis
oblectare animum subitamque avertere curam,
nec vitulorum aliae species per pabula laeta
365 derivare queunt animum curaque levare:
usque adeo quiddam proprium notumque requirit.
praeterea teneri tremulis cum vocibus haedi
cornigeras norunt matres agnique petulci
balantum pecudes: ita, quod natura reposcit,
370 ad sua quisque fere decurrunt ubera lactis.
postremo quodvis frumentum non tamen omne
quique suo genere inter se simile esse videbis,
quin intercurrat quaedam distantia formis.
concharumque genus parili ratione videmus
375 pingere telluris gremium, qua mollibus undis
litoris incurvi bibulam pavit aequor harenam.
quare etiam atque etiam simili ratione necessest,

natura quoniam constant neque facta manu sunt
unius ad certam formam primordia rerum,
dissimili inter se quaedam volitare figura.   380
  Perfacile est animi ratione exsolvere nobis
quare fulmineus multo penetralior ignis
quam noster fuat e taedis terrestribus ortus.
dicere enim possis caelestem fulminis ignem
subtilem magis e parvis constare figuris   385
atque ideo transire foramina quae nequit ignis
noster hic e lignis ortus taedaque creatus.
praeterea lumen per cornum transit, at imber
respuitur. quare? nisi luminis illa minora
corpora sunt quam de quibus est liquor almus aquarum. 390
et quamvis subito per colum vina videmus
perfluere; at contra tardum cunctatur olivum,
aut quia nimirum maioribus est elementis
aut magis hamatis inter se perque plicatis,
atque ideo fit uti non tam diducta repente   395
inter se possint primordia singula quaeque
singula per cuiusque foramina permanare.
  Huc accedit uti mellis lactisque liquores
iucundo sensu linguae tractentur in ore;
at contra taetra absinthi natura ferique   400
centauri foedo pertorquent ora sapore;
ut facile agnoscas e levibus atque rotundis
esse ea quae sensus iucunde tangere possunt,
at contra quae amara atque aspera cumque videntur,
haec magis hamatis inter se nexa teneri   405
proptereaque solere vias rescindere nostris
sensibus introituque suo perrumpere corpus.

  After thus explaining the effect on taste of the differences in atomic shape, Lucretius goes on to show
that similar effects are also produced in the realms of

hearing, smell, sight, and feeling (pleasure and pain). But to follow him here a knowledge of the mechanism of hearing, etc. is necessary, and this he does not give us until Book IV.

II. 478–729. Although the atoms vary both in size and in shape, there are limits to their variety. There is a maximum and a minimum size. The number of different shapes, too, is limited, not infinite; though the number of atoms of any given shape is infinite. Earth, the mother of all earthly things, contains a rich abundance of the varieties of the atoms and by admixture of these is able to produce things so different as water, fire, crops, beasts, men.

II. 730–1022. The atoms have shape and size, but no secondary qualities such as colour. For if the atoms possess colour, how can we explain sudden changes of colour in a thing? "If the level waters of the ocean were made of sky-blue seeds, they could in no wise grow white." Change of colour is to be accounted for by differences of the position, arrangement, size, and shape of the atoms, owing to which different kinds of blows are struck upon the eye (here too Lucretius is anticipating Book IV), so that we perceive now blue, now white. The single atoms then must be colourless: in the same way they are without heat, sound, taste, smell. Lastly, it is false to suppose that the single atoms possess sensation. Lucretius demonstrates this by many proofs, finishing, as he often does, with a *reductio ad absurdum*. Suppose that each of the atoms composing a man's mind and soul itself possesses sensation. "You must think then that the atoms are shaken with quivering mirth and laugh aloud and sprinkle their face and cheeks with the dew of their tears."

At this point we must pause and ask a question with which Lucretius has failed to deal. What is the process by which atoms, colourless, tasteless, etc., combine so as to form compound bodies which do possess colour, taste, and so on? An answer to this question is an essential part of the system, and the probability is that Lucretius' answer to it has dropped out of the text (between II. 164 and 165). By a curious coincidence there is a similar gap in the general account given by Epicurus in his Letter to Herodotus, and our knowledge of the answer is therefore based on rather fragmentary evidence. But whatever the full answer may have been it is unlikely that it can have dealt satisfactorily with the great difficulties which arise.

The general outline of the Epicurean doctrine on this question appears to be as follows. Owing to differences of shape (including jagged, hooked, and suchlike shapes) the atoms gradually form clusters. The formation of things by such a process can easily be imagined. The atoms "entangled by their own close-locking shapes make the strong roots of rock and the brute bulk of iron".[1] Even in such close-packed unions the motion of the atoms continues; they continue to vibrate or oscillate with infinitesimal trajectories, until very gradually (or suddenly, owing to an outside blow) they are loosed; and for this reason "change and decay in all around we see"—even in rocks. But what is it that gives the compound body its identity, that renders it distinct from its neighbours and from the free atoms all about it? Lucretius speaks of the "linking on of movements" (*consociare motus*[2]) by the atoms. "It is just this harmony of movement which constitutes the unity of the 'thing' and distinguishes it from external things and independent atoms."[3] This is but a vague conception, and, though we cannot condemn Epicurus

[1] II. 102–104.   [2] II. 111.   [3] B. p. 348.

and Lucretius unheard, there is little doubt that we see here a weak point in the structure of the system.

The next question is closely related to this. How is it that the compound bodies come to possess qualities that the individual atoms do not possess? How for instance do living creatures come to possess sensation when none of their component atoms possesses it? We can only answer these questions by saying that the group of atoms composing the compound body, the "organism", is something more than the mere aggregate of the individual component atoms. As an organism, the group of atoms acquires qualities and faculties not possessed by the single atoms: in the phrase of modern philosophy, there is a transition of quantity into quality. Lucretius may have wished to bring this out by the word he chose to describe the group of atoms forming a compound body: *concilium*.[1] This word is used by all other Latin authors always to

---

[1] A much more expressive word than the corresponding word used by Epicurus: σύστημα. *Concilium* raises the interesting question of Lucretius' use of metaphor in order to express scientific concepts. Besides *concilium*, other metaphors of his, drawn from life to express concepts about inanimate things, are drawn largely from characteristic activities of Roman life, e.g. *nexus*, *foedus*, *imperium*. No doubt he was partly forced to use such metaphors by the *patrii sermonis egestas* of which he complains: Latin was only beginning to evolve a philosophic and scientific vocabulary. But such metaphors have a special purpose in emphasizing a theme which runs through his whole work: the unity of the universe. Living and inanimate things alike are made of the same stuff and obey the same fundamental laws. Thus Lucretius' metaphors, whether used of necessity or by choice, have a special poetic value in stimulating us to be aware of the oneness of things and in emphasizing the unity of his poem. For an interesting discussion of Lucretius' use of metaphor see H. S. Davies' article in the *Criterion*, Oct. 1931.

describe a gathering of *people*, never a gathering of *things*. We all know that in a crowd the emotions of the individuals composing it tend to be intensified, so that the crowd will behave in a quite different way from the way in which the individuals by themselves would behave. A crowd is in fact something more than, something different from, the mere aggregate of individuals composing it. The word *concilium* then suggests an analogy which both illustrates and supports the Epicurean theory of the process by which compound bodies come to possess the qualities and faculties which, as we know from the evidence of our senses, they do possess. For these qualities and faculties are to an Epicurean really inherent in things: by the first law of Canonic we are debarred from supposing that such qualities only exist as subjective changes in our sensations.

We may still justifiably complain that Lucretius has suggested only an analogy, not an explanation. Looking at the question from the Epicurean point of view we see that Epicurus was confronted with two apparently irreconcilable facts, both vouched for by the infallible senses. On the one hand the senses tell us of the existence of qualities in things: therefore these qualities must exist. On the other hand the mind, "projecting itself" upon the evidence of the senses, is forced to the concept of the atom without colour, sensation and suchlike qualities. To reconcile the two facts by an adequate explanation may be impossible, but that they are facts is established by the fundamental principles of Canonic. Thus they remain as two essential parts of the Epicurean building, although the architect is unable to design anything better than a rather insubstantial rope-ladder as a means of getting from one to the other.

II. 1023–1174. We can now return to the second book at the point where we left it in order to discuss the problem which is not dealt with in the text as we have it.

Lucretius ends the second book as follows. Besides our "world"[1] there are other worlds in the universe, since the ever-whirling atoms must of necessity come together here and there into other such gatherings. This (Lucretius implies) prepares our minds for his final point: namely, that the world has gradually grown by increment of atoms, just as living creatures continue to grow till they reach their prime. "Then little by little age breaks their powers and their full-grown strength, and wastes away on the downhill path." The world is already past her prime; she is losing more atoms than she is receiving; and is on the path of decay which will lead to her ultimate dissolution.

This appears at first sight to be not directly relevant to the general subject of the second book. But it is intended no doubt as an illustration of a relevant point which Lucretius has not explicitly stated: namely, that a compound body is not composed of the same group of atoms throughout its period of existence, but is continually scattering some of its atoms abroad and garnering others in. There is "a continual renewal of substance in the compound by means of the counterplay of loss and gain, and it would almost be true to say that, in the Epicurean complex, form is the element of permanence rather than matter".[2]

[The close of the second book seems also to provide an easy transition to the subjects taken up in the fifth

---

[1] Our "world" (*mundus*) includes earth, sun, moon, stars, and the ether. The ether is a layer of fiery substance (*flammantia moenia mundi*) encircling the world, which is spherical, with the earth at the centre. Innumerable other "worlds" both of similar and of different types exist in the universe, separated by the *intermundia*, the intermundane expanses. See Book **v**.   [2] B. p. 351.

book. "For what remains", writes Lucretius in his introduction to the fifth book, "the train of my reasoning has now brought me to this point, that I must give account how the world is made of mortal body and also came to birth."[1] He forthwith proceeds to demonstrate by proofs that the world is mortal, and then to describe the manner of its birth. This follows naturally on from the subjects discussed in the second book. The fifth book next goes on to a discussion of astronomical questions, followed by an account of the origin of life and the famous description of the development of mankind from a primitive to a civilized condition. All this, we might justifiably suppose, leads up to the question of the nature of the soul and the nature of sensation and thought.

Thus the order of the books as they stand is surprising. The third book plunges straight into a description of the nature of the soul. The latter part of the book, in which Lucretius magnificently declaims against the folly of the fear of death, is the climax of the whole of the *de R. N.* The fourth book is a development of the third, explaining in detail the operations of the mind, soul, and senses: just as the sixth book is a development of the fifth, explaining in detail various special phenomena, first celestial, then terrestrial (e.g. thunder, earthquakes, etc.). We should expect Books v and vi to come immediately after Book ii and before Books iii and iv.

Perhaps Lucretius was in haste to come to his main message, the lesson which interested him most, namely, the mortality of the soul and the folly of the fear of death. Perhaps he would have changed the order of the books had he lived to complete and revise his work. We can only conjecture what the reason may have been;

[1] v. 64–66.

but in following his exposition from now on we must bear in mind that we have departed from a strictly logical order of topics.]

B (c) *The Soul.* Book III

III. 94–176. In the following passage Lucretius enters upon his account of the Soul. The Soul is a part of the body, wholly material: it is not, as some have maintained, a "harmony" or qualitative state of the body.

Having stated this Lucretius proceeds to explain the Epicurean distinction between (1) "mind" = *animus* = τὸ λογικὸν τῆς ψυχῆς, the seat of active thinking and willing, and (2) "soul"[1] = *anima* = τὸ ἄλογον τῆς ψυχῆς, that which gives life to the body and is the seat of sensation. Both alike are composed of material atoms, but the atoms composing *animus* are situated all in a group in the breast, while those composing *anima* are scattered at intervals throughout the body. The two are inseparably connected, for any violent disturbance of *animus* affects *anima* and eventually the body too.

In the following lines Lucretius assumes the distinction between *animus* and *anima* at first (ll. 94–135), although he does not explain the distinction till ll. 136 ff. Elsewhere in the *de R. N.* he sometimes makes the words *animus* and *anima* bear their distinct meanings: sometimes he uses either indiscriminately to distinguish "mind" and/or "soul" from "body". In translating it is important to remember that he is inconsistent in his use of these terms.

---

[1] In this account of Book III I have used soul = *anima*, Soul = *animus* + *anima*.

9. III. 94–160

Primum animum dico, mentem quam saepe vocamus, 94
in quo consilium vitae regimenque locatum est,
esse hominis partem nilo minus ac manus et pes
atque oculi partes animantis totius exstant.

*   *   *   *   *   *

sensum animi certa non esse in parte locatum,
verum habitum quendam vitalem corporis esse,
harmoniam Grai quam dicunt, quod faciat nos   100
vivere cum sensu, nulla cum in parte siet mens;
ut bona saepe valetudo cum dicitur esse
corporis, et non est tamen haec pars ulla valentis.
sic animi sensum non certa parte reponunt;
magno opere in quo mi diversi errare videntur.   105
saepe itaque in promptu corpus quod cernitur aegret,
cum tamen ex alia laetamur parte latenti;
et retro fit uti contra sit saepe vicissim,
cum miser ex animo laetatur corpore toto;
non alio pacto quam si, pes cum dolet aegri,   110
in nullo caput interea sit forte dolore.
praeterea molli cum somno dedita membra
effusumque iacet sine sensu corpus onustum,
est aliud tamen in nobis quod tempore in illo
multimodis agitatur et omnis accipit in se   115
laetitiae motus et curas cordis inanis.

Nunc animam quoque ut in membris cognoscere possis
esse neque harmonia corpus sentire solere,
principio fit uti detracto corpore multo
saepe tamen nobis in membris vita moretur;   120
atque eadem rursum, cum corpora pauca caloris
diffugere forasque per os est editus aer,
deserit extemplo venas atque ossa relinquit;
noscere ut hinc possis non aequas omnia partis
corpora habere neque ex aequo fulcire salutem,   125

sed magis haec, venti quae sunt calidique vaporis
semina, curare in membris ut vita moretur.
est igitur calor ac ventus vitalis in ipso
corpore qui nobis moribundos deserit artus.
130   Quapropter quoniam est animi natura reperta
atque animae quasi pars hominis, redde harmoniai
nomen, ad organicos alto delatum Heliconi;
sive aliunde ipsi porro traxere et in illam
transtulerunt, proprio quae tum res nomine egebat.
135 quidquid id est, habeant: tu cetera percipe dicta.
    Nunc animum atque animam dico coniuncta teneri
inter se atque unam naturam conficere ex se,
sed caput esse quasi et dominari in corpore toto
consilium quod nos animum mentemque vocamus.
140 idque situm media regione in pectoris haeret.
hic exsultat enim pavor ac metus, haec loca circum
laetitiae mulcent; hic ergo mens animusquest.
cetera pars animae per totum dissita corpus
paret et ad numen mentis momenque movetur.
145 idque sibi solum per se sapit, id sibi gaudet,
cum neque res animam neque corpus commovet una.
et quasi, cum caput aut oculus temptante dolore
laeditur in nobis, non omni concruciamur
corpore, sic animus nonnumquam laeditur ipse
150 laetitiaque viget, cum cetera pars animai
per membra atque artus nulla novitate cietur.
verum ubi vementi magis est commota metu mens,
consentire animam totam per membra videmus
sudoresque ita palloremque exsistere toto
155 corpore et infringi linguam vocemque aboriri,
caligare oculos, sonere auris, succidere artus,
denique concidere ex animi terrore videmus
saepe homines; facile ut quivis hinc noscere possit
esse animam cum animo coniunctam, quae cum animi vi
160 percussast, exim corpus propellit et icit.

III. 177–230. The speed with which the mind and
soul work shows that the atoms of which they are composed must be exceptionally small and smooth and
round. The thinness of the texture of these atoms is
further shown by the fact that at death the departure
of mind and soul makes no apparent difference in the
shape or weight of the body.

III. 231–322. In the following passage Lucretius goes
on to analyse the composition of the mind and soul.

Both *animus* and *anima* are made up of four components, wind (*aura* or *ventus*), heat (*calor* or *vapor*),
air (*aer*), and a fourth nameless substance (*quarta
natura*). Lucretius is less cautious than Epicurus, who
described the first three components as *like* wind, etc.
The fourth component is "nameless" not because there
is anything mysterious or transcendental about it, but
because there is no known substance sufficiently mobile
and fine to afford a means of describing it. It is of
course purely material like the other three. The point
of the distinction between "wind" and "air" is not
altogether clear. The most probable explanation is that
the wind-element is viewed as the cause of motion, and
the air-element as the cause of rest.

Sensation begins with the *quarta natura* and is passed
on by it to its fellow-components and then to the whole
body. A blow on the nose, for instance, results in the
disturbance of the *quarta natura* present in that part
of the *anima* situated at the point struck: the sensation
is passed on to the other *anima*-atoms of heat, wind, air
(in that order), and then to the atoms of the body.
The central *animus* being in close touch with the *anima*
receives the sensation instantaneously via the *quarta
natura* of the *animus*.

The four components are inextricably mixed, forming
one substance. The *quarta natura* is related to the other
three as the mind and soul are to the body. It is "the
Soul of the Soul". The three other elements vary in

importance: now one, now another predominates according to the nature of the individual or of the
occasion. Heat predominates in anger, wind in fear,
air in a mood of tranquillity. Varieties of temperament
are explicable in this way.

*10. III. 231–322

231   Nec tamen haec simplex nobis natura putanda est.
tenvis enim quaedam moribundos deserit aura
mixta vapore, vapor porro trahit aera secum.
nec calor est quisquam, cui non sit mixtus et aer.
235 rara quod eius enim constat natura, necessest
aeris inter eum primordia multa moveri.
iam triplex animi est igitur natura reperta;
nec tamen haec sat sunt ad sensum cuncta creandum,
nil horum quoniam recipit mens posse creare
240 sensiferos motus †quaedamque mente volutat†.
quarta quoque his igitur quaedam natura necessest
attribuatur. east omnino nominis expers;
qua neque mobilius quicquam neque tenvius exstat,
nec magis e parvis et levibus ex elementis;
245 sensiferos motus quae didit prima per artus.
prima cietur enim, parvis perfecta figuris;
inde calor motus et venti caeca potestas
accipit, inde aer; inde omnia mobilitantur,
concutitur sanguis, tum viscera persentiscunt
250 omnia, postremis datur ossibus atque medullis
sive voluptas est sive est contrarius ardor.
nec temere huc dolor usque potest penetrare neque acre
permanare malum, quin omnia perturbentur
usque adeo ut vitae desit locus atque animai
255 diffugiant partes per caulas corporis omnis.
sed plerumque fit in summo quasi corpore finis
motibus: hanc ob rem vitam retinere valemus.

Nunc ea quo pacto inter sese mixta quibusque
compta modis vigeant rationem reddere aventem
abstrahit invitum patrii sermonis egestas; 260
sed tamen, ut potero summatim attingere, tangam.
inter enim cursant primordia principiorum
motibus inter se, nil ut secernier unum
possit nec spatio fieri divisa potestas,
sed quasi multae vis unius corporis exstant. 265
quod genus in quovis animantum viscere vulgo
est odor et quidam calor et sapor, et tamen ex his
omnibus est unum perfectum corporis augmen.
sic calor atque aer et venti caeca potestas
mixta creant unam naturam et mobilis illa 270
vis, initum motus ab se quae dividit ollis,
sensifer unde oritur primum per viscera motus.
nam penitus prorsum latet haec natura subestque
nec magis hac infra quicquam est in corpore nostro
atque anima est animae proporro totius ipsa. 275
quod genus in nostris membris et corpore toto
mixta latens animi vis est animaeque potestas,
corporibus quia de parvis paucisque creatast.
sic tibi nominis haec expers vis facta minutis
corporibus latet atque animae quasi totius ipsa 280
proporrost anima et dominatur corpore toto.
consimili ratione necessest ventus et aer
et calor inter se vigeant commixta per artus
atque aliis aliud subsit magis emineatque
ut quiddam fieri videatur ab omnibus unum, 285
ni calor ac ventus sorsum sorsumque potestas
aeris interimant sensum diductaque solvant.
est etiam calor ille animo, quem sumit, in ira
cum fervescit et ex oculis micat acrius ardor.
est et frigida multa comes formidinis aura 290
quae ciet horrorem membris et concitat artus.

est etiam quoque pacati status aeris ille,
pectore tranquillo qui fit vultuque sereno.
sed calidi plus est illis quibus acria corda
295 iracundaque mens facile effervescit in ira.
quo genere in primis vis est violenta leonum,
pectora qui fremitu rumpunt plerumque gementes
nec capere irarum fluctus in pectore possunt.
at ventosa magis cervorum frigida mens est
300 et gelidas citius per viscera concitat auras
quae tremulum faciunt membris exsistere motum.
at natura boum placido magis aere vivit,
nec nimis irai fax umquam subdita percit
fumida, suffundens caecae caliginis umbra,
305 nec gelidis torpet telis perfixa pavoris:
interutrasque sitast, cervos saevosque leones.
sic hominum genus est. quamvis doctrina politos
constituat pariter quosdam, tamen illa relinquit
naturae cuiusque animi vestigia prima.
310 nec radicitus evelli mala posse putandumst,
quin proclivius hic iras decurrat ad acris,
ille metu citius paulo temptetur, at ille
tertius accipiat quaedam clementius aequo.
inque aliis rebus multis differre necessest
315 naturas hominum varias moresque sequaces;
quorum ego nunc nequeo caecas exponere causas
nec reperire figurarum tot nomina quot sunt
principiis, unde haec oritur variantia rerum.
illud in his rebus video firmare potesse,
320 usque adeo naturarum vestigia linqui
parvula quae nequeat ratio depellere nobis,
ut nil impediat dignam dis degere vitam.

How, we may ask, do the atoms of the *quarta natura*,
which as individual atoms do not possess the power of
thought or sensation, come to originate thought and

sensation? The answer is to be found in the Epicurean conception of the *concilium* of atoms, which was discussed on pp. 36, 37. The *quarta natura* is a *concilium* of exceedingly fine and smooth atoms, and as a *concilium* comes to possess qualities (the power of thought, the power of sensation) not possessed by the individual atoms. These qualities take effect when the atoms composing the *concilium* perform the appropriate motions: thought, sensation, etc. *are* in fact the motions made by the atoms of mind and soul.

III. 323–416. The Soul, being composed of exceedingly fine and smooth atoms, requires to be contained in some more solid structure if it is to escape dispersion, just as a liquid or a gas can only be held together in a containing vessel. The body then is the vessel of the Soul. In return the Soul gives to the body the sensation without which the body could not be said to live. Either therefore is wholly dependent on the other: neither can exist without the other.

The atoms of soul are scattered throughout the body at intervals which may be roughly measured by the size of the smallest things which, alighting on us, arouse sensation. "For sometimes we do not feel the clinging of dust on the body,...nor the slender threads of the spider that strike against us, when we are caught in its meshes as we move." Such things may alight *between* atoms of soul, without touching any one of them. The atoms of soul are scattered then at relatively distant intervals in all the pores of skin, blood, flesh, bone, etc.; soul-atoms and body-atoms alike being in constant motion, buffeting and being buffeted.

III. 417–829. Lucretius now takes up the main theme of the third book: the Soul is mortal. Like wave after wave comes a series of twenty-eight proofs of the Soul's mortality. Here we see his metrical technique at its

most effective: the cumulative weight of his hexameters
matches and intensifies the cumulative effect produced
by his battery of proofs.

The proofs are not arranged in careful order:
Lucretius sets down one after another as it comes into
his head. The Soul, being made of smooth and minute
atoms, must, like water or smoke, be scattered abroad
when the containing vessel is shattered. Again, even
disease affects the mind: how therefore can the mind
remain unaffected by death? Again, parts of the body
when lopped off may be seen to continue for a time to
twitch: we must therefore admit that each part of the
body contains part of the Soul, and since the Soul can
be thus divided it cannot be immortal. Again, if the
Soul is immortal and entered the body from without
at birth, why have we no remembrance of previous
existence? Such are some of Lucretius' arguments.

III. 830–1094. "Nil igitur mors est ad nos neque
pertinet hilum." With this line Lucretius concludes
his train of proofs and begins his song of triumph over
vanquished death. Death is annihilation, and in death
there can be no more pain nor desire of life. Therefore
fear of death is folly.

This passage, the climax of the *de R. N.*, is not concerned with the subject matter of Natural Science, but
rather with the logical effect of a knowledge of Natural
Science on our Ethical principles. In a systematized
account of Epicureanism, therefore, this passage must
be considered under the heading of Ethics (see pp. 88–
95).

B (d) *The Senses.* Book IV

[The fourth book is in a more disorganized state than
any of the preceding books and there is little doubt that
Lucretius would have re-arranged parts of it had he

lived to put his work into its final shape. There are
several passages which are clearly later additions made
by Lucretius to an earlier draft and inserted in such
a way as to interrupt his earlier line of thought. Even
apart from these the whole book is more rambling than
any of the preceding books.]

In Book III we have learned that the Soul is a collection of atoms which, as a *concilium*, possess sensation.
Book IV is concerned with the question arising out of
this, namely, how do the senses work? Lucretius has
already foreshadowed the general nature of his answer
in a passage in Book II: "For touch, touch by the holy
godheads! is the sense of the body."[1] The emphatic
way in which he makes this statement is suggestive of
the importance of this question to the whole system.
If we are to maintain a thorough-going Materialism we
must at all costs exclude any conception of things acting
upon our senses from a distance by some occult means:
we must explain their action not by occult conceptions
but in terms of the motion of matter. Outside objects
can arouse sensation in our Soul-atoms only by direct
impact. In other words all the senses are ultimately
reducible to the sense of touch.

IV. 26–109. Lucretius begins by attempting to explain sight. He at once reveals the intimate connection
which in his mind existed between this problem and
the problem nearest his heart, namely the problem of
death. Men sometimes dream of those who are dead,
and, unless they understand the nature of sight (both
physical and mental), this may tempt them to believe
that there is a life after death. Here is another illustration of a point already noted,[2] the strange importance
which Lucretius attached to dreams of the dead.

Having thus shown the relevance of the problem to

[1] II. 434, 435.   [2] I. 132 n. (Passage 1).

SL   4

his main theme, Lucretius proceeds to expound the
Epicurean theory of "Idols" (εἴδωλα = *simulacra*). In
the following passage the nature of the Idols is briefly
explained, and their existence demonstrated from
analogies in the visible world around us.

Every object is continually throwing off from its
surface a rapid succession of inconceivably thin layers
of atoms. These, the Idols, travel through the air at
great speed, preserving the shape of the object from
which they come; and then by striking the eye in rapid
succession they produce sight.

Such a theory, far-fetched and unconvincing in itself,
may well be thought an unpromising theme for poetry,
but Lucretius succeeds in breathing life into it by the
apt and picturesque analogies which he draws from
everyday experience.

II. IV. 26–109

26   Sed quoniam docui cunctarum exordia rerum
      qualia sint et quam variis distantia formis
      sponte sua volitent aeterno percita motu,
      quoque modo possit res ex his quaeque creari,
30   atque animi quoniam docui natura quid esset
      et quibus e rebus cum corpore compta vigeret
      quove modo distracta rediret in ordia prima,
      nunc agere incipiam tibi, quod vementer ad has res
      attinet, esse ea quae rerum simulacra vocamus;
35   quae, quasi membranae summo de corpore rerum
      dereptae, volitant ultroque citroque per auras,
      atque eadem nobis vigilantibus obvia mentis
      terrificant atque in somnis, cum saepe figuras
      contuimur miras simulacraque luce carentum,
      quae nos horrifice languentis saepe sopore
      excierunt, ne forte animas Acherunte reamur
      effugere aut umbras inter vivos volitare

neve aliquid nostri post mortem posse relinqui,
cum corpus simul atque animi natura perempta
in sua discessum dederint primordia quaeque.   45
   Dico igitur rerum effigias tenuisque figuras
mittier ab rebus summo de corpore rerum,
quae quasi membranae vel cortex nominitandast,   50
quod speciem ac formam similem gerit eius imago
cuiuscumque cluet de corpore fusa vagari.
id licet hinc quamvis hebeti cognoscere corde.
principio quoniam mittunt in rebus apertis
corpora res multae, partim diffusa solute,   55
robora ceu fumum mittunt ignesque vaporem,
et partim contexta magis condensaque, ut olim
cum teretes ponunt tunicas aestate cicadae,
et vituli cum membranas de corpore summo
nascentes mittunt, et item cum lubrica serpens   60
exuit in spinis vestem; nam saepe videmus
illorum spoliis vepris volitantibus auctas.
quae quoniam fiunt, tenuis quoque debet imago
ab rebus mitti summo de corpore rerum.
nam cur illa cadant magis ab rebusque recedant   65
quam quae tenvia sunt, hiscendist nulla potestas;
praesertim cum sint in summis corpora rebus
multa minuta, iaci quae possint ordine eodem
quo fuerint et formai servare figuram,
et multo citius, quanto minus indupediri   70
pauca queunt et quae sunt prima fronte locata.
nam certe iacere ac largiri multa videmus,
non solum ex aito penitusque, ut diximus ante,
verum de summis ipsum quoque saepe colorem.
et vulgo faciunt id lutea russaque vela   75
et ferrugina, cum magnis intenta theatris
per malos vulgata trabesque trementia flutant.
namque ibi consessum caveai subter et omnem

scaenai speciem, patrum coetumque decorum
80 inficiunt coguntque suo fluitare colore.
   et quanto circum mage sunt inclusa theatri
   moenia, tam magis haec intus perfusa lepore
   omnia corrident correpta luce diei.
   ergo lintea de summo cum corpore fucum
85 mittunt, effigias quoque debent mittere tenvis
   res quaeque, ex summo quoniam iaculantur utraque.
   sunt igitur iam formarum vestigia certa
   quae vulgo volitant subtili praedita filo
   nec singillatim possunt secreta videri.
90 praeterea omnis odor fumus vapor atque aliae res
   consimiles ideo diffusae e rebus abundant,
   ex alto quia dum veniunt intrinsecus ortae,
   scinduntur per iter flexum, nec recta viarum
   ostia sunt qua contendant exire coortae.
95 at contra tenuis summi membrana coloris
   cum iacitur, nil est quod eam discerpere possit,
   in promptu quoniam est in prima fronte locata.
   postremo speculis in aqua splendoreque in omni
   quaecumque apparent nobis simulacra, necessest,
100 quandoquidem simili specie sunt praedita rerum,
    ex ea imaginibus missis consistere rerum.
104 sunt igitur tenues formae rerum similesque
105 effigiae, singillatim quas cernere nemo
    cum possit, tamen assiduo crebroque repulsu
    reiectae reddunt speculorum ex aequore visum,
    nec ratione alia servari posse videntur,
109 tanto opere ut similes reddantur cuique figurae.

   IV. 110–268. Lucretius proceeds to describe the
nature of the Idols in more detail. They are inconceivably thin; they stream away from the surface of an
object in exceedingly rapid succession; they move with
indescribable speed.

IV. 269–521. Next Lucretius tries to grapple with some of the peculiarities of sight and to explain them in terms of the Idols theory. His first subject is the mirror, which calls forth fifty of the most difficult lines in the whole poem. Their difficulty is due not so much to extreme profundity as to the fact that Lucretius seems to have had but an unsure grasp of the theory he puts forward. After the mirror he deals with peculiarities such as the eyes' avoidance of bright objects, and the way in which our shadow follows us about.

These topics naturally lead on to the question of optical illusions (Passage 3). After giving a number of examples of illusion Lucretius sets forth the fundamental principle of Epicureanism, the infallibility of the senses.

Lucretius fails to deal with some of the more important mechanical difficulties involved in the theory of Idols. For instance, do the Idols diminish in size as they travel through the air, and if not, how do the Idols of a large object enter our eyes? It is easy to make a formidable list of such difficulties; and all that can be said in defence of Epicurus' theory is that he was at least in advance of some other ancient philosophers (e.g. Plato), who held that vision was not due to something which left the object and entered the eye but to something which was projected from the eye and fell upon the object. Epicurus did grasp the right end of the stick, though it is difficult to imagine that his theory as it stands can have convinced anyone.

IV. 522–721. Lucretius deals with the other senses, hearing, taste, smell. The path here, he tells his reader, is "by no means stony". The other senses can more easily be reduced to the sense of touch than can the sense of sight. In a picturesque passage Lucretius explains how hearing is caused by particles of sound

which are emitted from the source of the sound and
travel outwards in all directions. When these particles
strike upon an obstacle, sometimes they are cast back,
and thus "among solitary places rocks give back the
counterparts of words each in due order, when we seek
our comrades wandering amid the dark hills, and with
loud voice summon them scattered here and there";
sometimes the particles pass through "the winding
pores in things", so that we hear a conversation through
closed doors.

Taste is produced by direct touch, the nature of the
taste depending on the smoothness or roughness of the
atoms composing the food or drink. Smell is caused
by atoms emanating from deep within the object rather
than from the surface.

IV. 722–822. Lucretius next attempts to explain the
process of thought, which he regards purely as visualization, i.e. mental sight. He deals here with only two
sides of his complex subject. (1) Thought (and dreams)
are sometimes caused by wandering Idols, finer than
those cast off by the objects which we actually see, and
capable of piercing through the pores of our body to
impinge directly on the atoms of the mind. These finer
Idols are everywhere about us and are continually
forming and combining. "For in truth the image of
the Centaur comes not from a living thing, since there
never was the nature of such a living creature, but when
by chance the images of man and horse have met, they
cling together readily at once." The Idols may outlast
the source whence they sprang, and thus we may dream
of the dead. (Of most importance in the class of finer
Idols are the Idols of the gods, but Lucretius does not
mention them here.) (2) How is it that we can immediately think of that which we wish to think of?
Lucretius touches on but does not deal fully with the

Epicurean theory of the mind's power of "projecting itself" upon the desired Idols.[1]

IV. 823–857. Here Lucretius breaks off his detailed scientific discourse in order to enunciate a general proposition of great importance to the whole Epicurean system. He denies the teleological view of the universe, that is, he denies that things were created for the purpose of their use, and sets forth the Epicurean doctrine that things (e.g. the eyes, the legs), having come into being by the blind combination of atoms, have developed the uses to which they are put. What he says is directed especially against the Final Cause of Aristotle and the Divine Providence of the Stoics, but the question he raises is one that may be said to split all systems of philosophy, ancient and modern, into two camps.

IV. 858–1287. The following paragraphs deal with topics clearly connected with the main subject of Book IV, although the selection and the order of the topics are rather puzzling. Lucretius explains in terms of the movement of the atoms in our bodies (1) eating, (2) walking, as an illustration of the operation of the will, (3) sleeping (with an excursus about dreams), (4) love and procreation.

The subject of love moves Lucretius once again to cease to write as a scientist, and to write as a moral philosopher. He devotes a long passage (ll. 1058–1191) to an attack on love.[2] His message is the cold doctrine of Epicurus: love causes disturbance to peace of mind, therefore avoid it. But Lucretius' tone is very different from that of his master: he writes of love with the penetration of a satirist and with the intensity of a lover.

[1] See the summary of Canonic, pp. 13–15. There is no need to point out the obvious deficiencies of Lucretius' account.

[2] See C 2 (c), p. 100.

Here once again we see the passion with which he
writes in strange contrast with the passionless state of
mind which he is advocating.

B (e) *Our World and its astronomical laws. The origin and development of man.* Book v

[The subjects discussed in Book v follow on naturally,
as we have seen,[1] from those discussed in Book II.]

v. 55–90. In addition to the usual preface in praise
of Epicurus, there is a further introductory passage
summarizing the subjects to be discussed in the course
of the fifth book.

v. 91–415. Lucretius takes up his first subject—the
same subject as that with which the second book
closed—namely, that the world *(mundus)*[2] is mortal and
will some day be utterly destroyed. Before he begins
to give detailed proofs of this statement he inserts a
long digression (ll. 110–234) in which he shows that
the world is not itself "of divine body", nor have the
gods had any hand in creating it.[3]

There follows an accumulation of proofs of the
mortality of the world, set forth in a manner that
reminds us of the relentless list of proofs of the soul's
mortality in Book III. The component substances of
the world (e.g. earth, water) are subject to the universal
processes of increase and decrease: therefore the world
too must be subject to the same processes.—"Moreover, if there was no birth and beginning of the earth
and sky, and they were always from everlasting, why
beyond the Theban war and the doom of Troy have
not other poets sung of other happenings as well?"
The world therefore had a birth.—The world might

[1] p. 38.
[2] For the meaning of *mundus* see p. 38.
[3] The Epicurean gods will be more fully discussed under
B (g).

be immortal if there were no room outside it into which
it could fall asunder, but in fact the world is surrounded
by infinite space waiting to swallow it up: "the gate
of death is not shut on sky or sun or earth or the deep
waters of the sea, but it stands open facing them with
huge vast gaping maw."—So the list of proofs goes on.

v. 416–563. Lucretius next gives a description of the
birth of this world, which was due to the blind motions
and combinations of the whirling atoms. His account
is dramatic and vivid and is a good instance of his
ability to make poetry of pseudo-science. Heavier
atoms met together and formed the Earth; lighter atoms
were squeezed out and formed the band of Ether
which encircles the world; atoms of intermediate weight
formed sun, moon, and stars, which float midway
between Earth and Ether. The world is spherical and
the Earth is at the centre of the world: how to account
for the manner in which it maintains its position was
a problem of great difficulty to Epicurus, who (in common with the ancient world in general) knew nothing
of the laws of the attraction of matter. Lucretius sets
forth an explanation that is ingenious rather than con-
vincing and need not detain us here.

v. 564–770.[1] Astronomy is naturally the next subject.
Parts of this section are interesting for the ingenuity
of the suggestions put forward,[2] but its chief interest
lies in the illustration it affords of the Epicurean attitude
of mind towards enquiries of this nature. We may
consider this under two headings.[3]

(1) The *purpose* of all Epicurean scientific enquiry

[1] A paragraph (ll. 509–533) in the preceding section deals
with the motions of the stars and would be more relevant
in the present section than in its actual context.

[2] On the technical side J. D. Duff's intro. to his ed. of
Book v is very helpful.

[3] See also the summary of Epicurean Canonic, pp. 6–17.

was the attainment of peace of mind through demon-
stration that everything can be accounted for by natural
causes; there is therefore no Supernatural to be feared.
Sometimes we cannot point to any one cause as *the*
cause. To the Epicurean, however, this is immaterial:
provided he can suggest a number of *possible* natural
causes his purpose—peace of mind—is achieved. "To
affirm which of the causes it is, is in no wise the task
of one treading forward step by step" (ll. 532–533).
In this section therefore, where Lucretius is discussing
phenomena whose causes are beyond the reach of our
sense-perception (e.g. the motions of the stars, the
alternation of day and night), he is content to lay down
not one but a number of alternative possible suggestions. The scientist would wish to enquire further, but
the Epicurean was interested in natural science not for
its own sake but as the handmaid of ethics.

(2) The *method* of Epicurean enquiry in fields such
as Astronomy is also interesting. The ultimate court
of appeal is the Senses. When we enquire into astronomical phenomena our senses can tell us what the
facts are (e.g. we can observe exactly the motions of
the stars), but the *causes* are hidden from our senses.
The best method of approach then is by analogy: we
must seek for analogous phenomena the causes of which
can be observed by the senses. This is the method
which has led and leads science forward "step by step"
to the light of knowledge. But there is always the
danger of introducing a false analogy, and in the following passage we see that Epicurus could be led sadly
astray by analogies as false as they are plausible.

If we consider the question, What is the size of sun,
moon, and stars? we must, as always, start from the
evidence of the senses. Our eyes tell us that they are
very small. If we were considering distant objects on
the earth we could approach closer to them and get
clearer direct evidence from our senses: but in con-

sidering the heavenly bodies we can only argue in-
directly, from analogy. (i) Take as example a fire which
we see on earth: if we are sufficiently near to it to
feel its heat, its actual size cannot be much greater than
its apparent size. Now we can feel the heat of the sun:
therefore the sun must be about the size it appears to
be. (ii) If a thing on earth is very distant we see it
with blurred edges. But the moon is clear-cut: therefore it cannot be sufficiently distant to be much smaller
in appearance than it is in reality.—In this way Epicurus
was led to conclusions which appeared ridiculous even
to his contemporaries, for many ancient philosophers
grasped the truth that the sun is much greater than
the earth.

*12. v. 564–591

Nec nimio solis maior rota nec minor ardor   564
esse potest, nostris quam sensibus esse videtur.
nam quibus e spatiis cumque ignes lumina possunt
adicere et calidum membris adflare vaporem,
nil illa his intervallis de corpore libant
flammarum, nil ad speciem est contractior ignis.
proinde, calor quoniam solis lumenque profusum   570
perveniunt nostros ad sensus et loca mulcent,
forma quoque hinc solis debet filumque videri,
nil adeo ut possis plus aut minus addere, vere.
lunaque sive notho fertur loca lumine lustrans   575
sive suam proprio iactat de corpore lucem,
quidquid id est, nilo fertur maiore figura
quam, nostris oculis qua cernimus, esse videtur.
nam prius omnia, quae longe semota tuemur
aera per multum, specie confusa videntur   580
quam minui filum. quapropter luna necesse est,
quandoquidem claram speciem certamque figuram
praebet, ut est oris extremis cumque notata,

quantaque quantast, hinc nobis videatur in alto.
585 postremo quoscumque vides hinc aetheris ignis;
quandoquidem quoscumque in terris cernimus ignis,
dum tremor est clarus, dum cernitur ardor eorum,
perparvum quiddam interdum mutare videntur
alteram utram in partem filum, quo longius absunt:
590 scire licet perquam pauxillo posse minores
esse vel exigua maiores parte brevique.

v. 772–924. "For the rest," Lucretius writes, "since
I have unfolded in what manner each thing could take
place throughout the blue vault of the great world,...
now I return to the youth of the world, and the soft
fields of Earth, and what first with new power of
creation they resolved to raise into the coasts of light
and entrust to the gusty winds." He describes first
the birth of vegetable life on the Earth, and then the
birth of living creatures.

The origin of life presented less of a problem to the
ancient world than it does to us. Virgil's advice to the
bee-keeper (G. IV. 281 ff.), that if his stock of bees
fails him he should generate a fresh swarm from the
rotting carcase of a bullock, is only one of many
references in ancient literature to the generally-held
belief in spontaneous generation. Lucretius has already
referred to the birth of worms from mud (II. 928 and
871): here he refers to it again. Since Earth, now in
her old age, can still produce living creatures, we need
not wonder that in her lusty youth she produced birds
and animals by spontaneous generation. She is truly
called the mother of all things. Throughout this passage
Lucretius writes of the Earth in language that is appropriate to a human mother and so once again emphasizes
the unity of animate and inanimate matter.[1]

The *naïveté* of this account of the origin of life is

[1] See pp. 30, 31 and p. 36 n. 1.

in strong contrast with the perspicuity of the lines
which follow next, foreshadowing the modern theories
of Evolution and Natural Selection. Earth at first produced many monstrosities and indeed whole species
that were not adapted to their surroundings. "These
fell a prey and spoil to others, all entangled in the
fateful trammels of their own being, until nature
brought their kind to destruction."

v. 925–1457. We now enter upon one of the most
notable passages in the *de R. N.*, where both the intel-
lectual and the imaginative power of Lucretius have
free play. His subject is the development of mankind
from primitive savagery to civilization.

Religion and the idea of progress are not easily com-
patible. Most religions have pre-supposed a divine
creation of the world, and must therefore explain the
evil that we find in the world as the result of a decadence
from a higher state. In strong contrast to this is the
view of those who would explain the good that we find
in the world as the result of a slow process of evolution.
The belief in a past Golden Age was an essential part
of the Greco-Roman pagan religion; and the practice
of worshipping ancestors and heroes shows that religion
directed men's minds to the past as being the period
when man was nearer God.[1] Epicurus attacked religion
at this point as at all other points. In opposition to the
prevalent belief he put forward the idea of progress,
the idea that the civilized life of mankind in com-

[1] The belief in a Golden Age was to some extent reconciled
with the fact of material progress in the Prometheus legend.
The popular view of mankind's past was doubtless extremely
vague and confused. Apart from the writings of philosophers, passages of considerable interest are Eur. *Suppl.*
201 ff. and Soph. *Ant.* 332 ff., in addition of course to Hesiod
and the *P.V.* of Aesch. Cf. too Hor. *Od.* III. vi. 45 ff.
and Virg. *Ecl.* IV.

munities was the result of a slow process of development from the savage and lonely life of a wild beast.

(In saying that Epicurus put forward the idea of
progress we must be careful to guard against any con-
fusion of his views with the view of progress held by
many in the modern world. "Progress" means to them
a steady advance which has been made and will continue to be made by mankind towards an infinitely
distant goal of perfection in body, mind and spirit.
Epicurus was not an optimist in this sense; his views
differed from this optimistic view of progress in two
ways: (1) The development of man's intelligence, sensi-
tivity, etc., has not been an unmixed blessing from
the Epicurean point of view, for the number of man's
wants has increased together with the number of his
pleasures, and it is therefore doubtful to what extent
true Epicurean pleasure has been increased.[1] (2) The
possibilities of progress in the future are limited, for
the world like every other organism will come to an
end, and, since there are many signs that the world
is already old (Book II *fin.*), the end is probably not
far distant. In any case the future is of no concern to
the Epicurean, beyond his own lifetime.)

In the time of Epicurus there was little information
about the distant past or about contemporary peoples
still in a primitive state. But in spite of the lack of data
Epicurus, by using what information there was and
through observation of and inference from the habits
of his fellow-men, arrived at conclusions about the
history of mankind which (sometimes even in detail)
are in close accord with the conclusions of modern
science. Passage 13 contains a considerable part of
Lucretius' account, and raises a number of general
questions of great importance. These will be touched
on in the following summary in the order in which they

[1] See v. 1408 ff., esp. 1430–1433; VI. 9 ff.

occur. Lucretius' account does not follow a logical order and it is clear that this part of his work too would have been revised had he lived.

(925–987) Primitive life was hard and brutish. Lucretius at once disposes of the idea of a Golden Age and he has no illusions about the life of the "noble savage".

(988–1010) Primitive man was comparatively defenceless and death was frequent. But they did not have to run modern risks, e.g. large-scale battles and shipwrecks. "Then, want of food would give over their drooping limbs to death; now, on the other hand, 'tis surfeit of good things brings them low." Lucretius here emphasizes the Epicurean view that material progress has produced many obstacles as well as aids to man's true welfare.

(1011–1027) The complete egoism of primitive man was first tempered by family affection. This led in turn to mutual compacts between neighbours *nec laedere nec violari*. This important passage briefly states the theory of the Social Contract. In contradiction of Aristotle's theory, man is *not* naturally a political animal: as a matter of historical fact, according to Epicurus, man only comes to live in communities because he realizes the selfish advantages to be gained from doing so. This doctrine is of fundamental importance to the whole question of Ethics, for it pre-supposes that there can be no absolute, still less any divinely-instituted, system of social morality. The only system of social morality is that which has been arrived at by agreement between men for their own individual convenience.[1]

(1028–1090) This passage deals with the question of the origin of language, a question much discussed by ancient philosophers. Was the origin of language due to φύσις, "nature", or θέσις, "deliberation"?

[1] See C 2 (a), p. 96.

Epicurus was sufficiently acute to see that the most likely solution lay in a compromise: language originally arose from the natural instinct to make various noises to indicate various feelings or things, but at a later stage "deliberation" played a part in the making of accurate distinctions between words and in the invention of new words. In this he agrees with Darwin.— Lucretius here summarizes the Epicurean theory at the outset (see ll. 1028–9 and n.); but in the rest of the passage he contents himself with emphasizing only the first stage, the *natural* origin of language, by dwelling on the way in which children and animals instinctively express themselves by various sounds.

(1091–1104) Lucretius goes back to the question of the origin of the use of fire, which he had already assumed in a previous paragraph (l. 1011). Mankind first acquired fire from lightning or from the chance rubbing of trees upon one another. The thought underlying this and the following paragraphs is the substitution of natural for divine causation. (In the popular belief fire was brought down from heaven by Prometheus.)

(1105–1135) Exceptionally gifted men introduced advances in civilization, and kings and rich men made their appearance. (The stories of god-descended heroes and kings, Lucretius implies, are false.) The resulting struggle for honour and wealth leads Lucretius to re-affirm the Epicurean ideal of the quiet life and contentment with a little.

(1136–1160) The overthrow of monarchy (Lucretius is thinking of Roman history) and the consequent anarchy led men to agree to the establishment of laws. Here we have the Social Contract in a more advanced form. Lucretius proceeds to voice one of the principles of Epicurean ethics, that the only valid reason for acting justly is the fear of punishment.[1]

[1] See C 2 (*a*), p. 96.

(1161–1240) The origin of religion is the next subject
—a subject of special importance to the Epicurean
system. It is due to natural, not divine, causation.
Lucretius puts forward two explanations: (1) (1161–
1182) Continually recurring visions of beings of super-
human size and beauty led men to believe that the gods
existed and that they were immortal. (These visions,
according to the Epicurean theory, must be caused by
Idols thrown off by material objects, and the gods
therefore must exist in material form, but they have
no connection or concern with mankind.[1]) (2) (1183–
1240) Ignorance about the causes of celestial phenomena and of all the manifestations of the great forces
of nature has led men to suppose that the gods were
responsible, and that these gods lived in the sky. In
his noble description of the forces of nature Lucretius
reveals that as a poet, if not as a philosopher, he too
felt the urge to believe in the working of a divine power
behind it all.[2]

13. V. 925–1240

At genus humanum multo fuit illud in arvis   925
durius, ut decuit, tellus quod dura creasset,
et maioribus et solidis magis ossibus intus
fundatum, validis aptum per viscera nervis,
nec facile ex aestu nec frigore quod caperetur
nec novitate cibi nec labi corporis ulla.   930
multaque per caelum solis volventia lustra
vulgivago vitam tractabant more ferarum.
nec robustus erat curvi moderator aratri
quisquam, nec scibat ferro molirier arva
nec nova defodere in terram virgulta neque altis   935
arboribus veteres decidere falcibu' ramos.
quod sol atque imbres dederant, quod terra crearat
sponte sua, satis id placabat pectora donum.

[1] See B (g), p. 78.   [2] See Intro. pp. xxi ff.

glandiferas inter curabant corpora quercus
940 plerumque; et quae nunc hiberno tempore cernis
arbuta puniceo fieri matura colore,
plurima tum tellus etiam maiora ferebat.
multaque praeterea novitas tum florida mundi
pabula dura tulit, miseris mortalibus ampla.
945 at sedare sitim fluvii fontesque vocabant,
ut nunc montibus e magnis decursus aquai
claru' citat late sitientia saecla ferarum.
denique nota vagi silvestria templa tenebant
nympharum, quibus e scibant umori' fluenta
950 lubrica proluvie larga lavere umida saxa,
umida saxa, super viridi stillantia musco,
et partim plano scatere atque erumpere campo.
necdum res igni scibant tractare neque uti
pellibus et spoliis corpus vestire ferarum,
955 sed nemora atque cavos montis silvasque colebant
et frutices inter condebant squalida membra
verbera ventorum vitare imbrisque coacti.
nec commune bonum poterant spectare neque ullis
moribus inter se scibant nec legibus uti.
960 quod cuique obtulerat praedae fortuna, ferebat
sponte sua sibi quisque valere et vivere doctus.
et Venus in silvis iungebat corpora amantum;
conciliabat enim vel mutua quamque cupido
vel violenta viri vis atque impensa libido
965 vel pretium, glandes atque arbuta vel pira lecta.
et manuum mira freti virtute pedumque
consectabantur silvestria saecla ferarum
missilibus saxis et magno pondere clavae;
multaque vincebant, vitabant pauca latebris;
970 saetigerisque pares subus silvestria membra
nuda dabant terrae nocturno tempore capti,
circum se foliis ac frondibus involventes.

nec plangore diem magno solemque per agros
quaerebant pavidi palantes noctis in umbris,
sed taciti respectabant somnoque sepulti,   975
dum rosea face sol inferret lumina caelo.
a parvis quod enim consuerant cernere semper
alterno tenebras et lucem tempore gigni,
non erat ut fieri posset mirarier umquam
nec diffidere ne terras aeterna teneret   980
nox in perpetuum detracto lumine solis.
sed magis illud erat curae, quod saecla ferarum
infestam miseris faciebant saepe quietem.
eiectique domo fugiebant saxea tecta
spumigeri suis adventu validique leonis   985
atque intempesta cedebant nocte paventes
hospitibus saevis instrata cubilia fronde.
   Nec nimio tum plus quam nunc mortalia saecla
dulcia linquebant lamentis lumina vitae.
unus enim tum quisque magis deprensus eorum   990
pabula viva feris praebebat, dentibus haustus,
et nemora ac montis gemitu silvasque replebat
viva videns vivo sepeliri viscera busto.
at quos effugium servarat corpore adeso,
posterius tremulas super ulcera taetra tenentes   995
palmas horriferis accibant vocibus Orcum,
donec eos vita privarant vermina saeva
expertis opis, ignaros quid vulnera vellent.
at non multa virum sub signis milia ducta
una dies dabat exitio nec turbida ponti   1000
aequora lidebant navis ad saxa virosque.
hic temere incassum frustra mare saepe coortum
saevibat leviterque minas ponebat inanis,
nec poterat quemquam placidi pellacia ponti
subdola pellicere in fraudem ridentibus undis.   1005
improba navigii ratio tum caeca iacebat.

tum penuria deinde cibi languentia leto
membra dabat, contra nunc rerum copia mersat.
illi imprudentes ipsi sibi saepe venenum
1010 vergebant, nunc dant aliis sollertius ipsi.
     Inde casas postquam ac pellis ignemque pararunt,
et mulier coniuncta viro concessit in unum
          *   *   *   *   *   *   *
cognita sunt, prolemque ex se videre creatam,
tum genus humanum primum mollescere coepit.
1015 ignis enim curavit ut alsia corpora frigus
non ita iam possent caeli sub tegmine ferre,
et Venus imminuit viris puerique parentum
blanditiis facile ingenium fregere superbum.
tunc et amicitiem coeperunt iungere aventes
1020 finitimi inter se nec laedere nec violari,
et pueros commendarunt muliebreque saeclum,
vocibus et gestu cum balbe significarent
imbecillorum esse aequum misererier omnis.
nec tamen omnimodis poterat concordia gigni,
1025 sed bona magnaque pars servabat foedera caste;
aut genus humanum iam tum foret omne peremptum
nec potuisset adhuc perducere saecla propago.
     At varios linguae sonitus natura subegit
mittere et utilitas expressit nomina rerum,
1030 non alia longe ratione atque ipsa videtur
protrahere ad gestum pueros infantia linguae,
cum facit ut digito quae sint praesentia monstrent.
sentit enim vis quisque suas quoad possit abuti.
cornua nata prius vitulo quam frontibus exstent,
1035 illis iratus petit atque infestus inurget.
at catuli pantherarum scymnique leonum
unguibus ac pedibus iam tum morsuque repugnant,
vix etiam cum sunt dentes unguesque creati.
alituum porro genus alis omne videmus

fidere et a pinnis tremulum petere auxiliatum.   1040
proinde putare aliquem tum nomina distribuisse
rebus et inde homines didicisse vocabula prima,
desiperest. nam cur hic posset cuncta notare
vocibus et varios sonitus emittere linguae,
tempore eodem alii facere id non quisse putentur?   1045
praeterea si non alii quoque vocibus usi
inter se fuerant, unde insita notities est
utilitatis et unde data est huic prima potestas,
quid vellet facere ut sciret animoque videret?
cogere item pluris unus victosque domare   1050
non poterat, rerum ut perdiscere nomina vellent.
nec ratione docere ulla suadereque surdis,
quid sit opus facto, facilest; neque enim paterentur
nec ratione ulla sibi ferrent amplius auris
vocis inauditos sonitus obtundere frustra.   1055
postremo quid in hac mirabile tantoperest re,
si genus humanum, cui vox et lingua vigeret,
pro vario sensu varia res voce notaret?
cum pecudes mutae, cum denique saecla ferarum
dissimilis soleant voces variasque ciere,   1060
cum metus aut dolor est et cum iam gaudia gliscunt.
quippe etenim licet id rebus cognoscere apertis.
irritata canum cum primum magna Molossum
mollia ricta fremunt duros nudantia dentis,
longe alio sonitu rabie restricta minantur,   1065
et cum iam latrant et vocibus omnia complent.
at catulos blande cum lingua lambere temptant
aut ubi eos iactant pedibus morsuque petentes
suspensis teneros imitantur dentibus haustus,
longe alio pacto gannitu vocis adulant,   1070
et cum deserti baubantur in aedibus aut cum
plorantes fugiunt summisso corpore plagas.
denique non hinnitus item differre videtur,

inter equas ubi equus florenti aetate iuvencus
1075 pinnigeri saevit calcaribus ictus amoris
et fremitum patulis sub naribus edit ad arma,
et cum sic alias concussis artubus hinnit?
postremo genus alituum variaeque volucres,
accipitres atque ossifragae mergique marinis
1080 fluctibus in salso victum vitamque petentes,
longe alias alio iaciunt in tempore voces,
et cum de victu certant praedaque repugnant.
et partim mutant cum tempestatibus una
raucisonos cantus, cornicum ut saecla vetusta
1085 corvorumque greges ubi aquam dicuntur et imbris
poscere et interdum ventos aurasque vocare.
ergo si varii sensus animalia cogunt,
muta tamen cum sint, varias emittere voces,
quanto mortalis magis aequumst tum potuisse
1090 dissimilis alia atque alia res voce notare!
      Illud in his rebus tacitus ne forte requiras,
fulmen detulit in terram mortalibus ignem
primitus, inde omnis flammarum diditur ardor.
multa videmus enim caelestibus incita flammis
1095 fulgere, cum caeli donavit plaga vapore.
et ramosa tamen cum ventis pulsa vacillans
aestuat in ramos incumbens arboris arbor,
exprimitur validis extritus viribus ignis,
emicat interdum flammai fervidus ardor,
1100 mutua dum inter se rami stirpesque teruntur.
quorum utrumque dedisse potest mortalibus ignem.
inde cibum coquere ac flammae mollire vapore
sol docuit, quoniam mitescere multa videbant
verberibus radiorum atque aestu victa per agros.
1105   Inque dies magis hi victum vitamque priorem
commutare novis monstrabant rebus et igni
ingenio qui praestabant et corde vigebant.

condere coeperunt urbis arcemque locare
praesidium reges ipsi sibi perfugiumque,
et pecus atque agros divisere atque dedere 1110
pro facie cuiusque et viribus ingenioque;
nam facies multum valuit viresque vigebant.
posterius res inventast aurumque repertum,
quod facile et validis et pulchris dempsit honorem;
divitioris enim sectam plerumque sequuntur 1115
quamlibet et fortes et pulchro corpore creti.
quod siquis vera vitam ratione gubernet,
divitiae grandes homini sunt vivere parce
aequo animo; neque enim est umquam penuria parvi.
at claros homines voluerunt se atque potentis, 1120
ut fundamento stabili fortuna maneret
et placidam possent opulenti degere vitam,
nequiquam, quoniam ad summum succedere honorem
certantes iter infestum fecere viai,
et tamen e summo, quasi fulmen, deicit ictos 1125
invidia interdum contemptim in Tartara taetra;
invidia quoniam, ceu fulmine, summa vaporant
plerumque et quae sunt aliis magis edita cumque;
ut satius multo iam sit parere quietum
quam regere imperio res velle et regna tenere. 1130
proinde sine incassum defessi sanguine sudent,
angustum per iter luctantes ambitionis;
quandoquidem sapiunt alieno ex ore petuntque
res ex auditis potius quam sensibus ipsis,
nec magis id nunc est neque erit mox quam fuit ante. 1135
 Ergo regibus occisis subversa iacebat
pristina maiestas soliorum et sceptra superba,
et capitis summi praeclarum insigne cruentum
sub pedibus vulgi magnum lugebat honorem;
nam cupide conculcatur nimis ante metutum. 1140
res itaque ad summam faecem turbasque redibat,

imperium sibi cum ac summatum quisque petebat.
inde magistratum partim docuere creare
iuraque constituere, ut vellent legibus uti.
1145 nam genus humanum, defessum vi colere aevum,
ex inimicitiis languebat; quo magis ipsum
sponte sua cecidit sub leges artaque iura.
acrius ex ira quod enim se quisque parabat
ulcisci quam nunc concessumst legibus aequis,
1150 hanc ob rem est homines pertaesum vi colere aevum.
inde metus maculat poenarum praemia vitae.
circumretit enim vis atque iniuria quemque
atque, unde exortast, ad eum plerumque revertit,
nec facilest placidam ac pacatam degere vitam
1155 qui violat factis communia foedera pacis.
etsi fallit enim divum genus humanumque,
perpetuo tamen id fore clam diffidere debet;
quippe ubi se multi per somnia saepe loquentes
aut morbo delirantes protraxe ferantur
1160 et celata diu in medium peccata dedisse.
    Nunc quae causa deum per magnas numina gentis
pervulgarit et ararum compleverit urbis
suscipiendaque curarit sollemnia sacra,
quae nunc in magnis florent sacra rebu' locisque,
1165 unde etiam nunc est mortalibus insitus horror
qui delubra deum nova toto suscitat orbi
terrarum et festis cogit celebrare diebus,
non ita difficilest rationem reddere verbis.
quippe etenim iam tum divum mortalia saecla
1170 egregias animo facies vigilante videbant
et magis in somnis mirando corporis auctu.
his igitur sensum tribuebant propterea quod
membra movere videbantur vocesque superbas
mittere pro facie praeclara et viribus amplis.
1175 aeternamque dabant vitam, quia semper eorum

suppeditabatur facies et forma manebat,
et tamen omnino quod tantis viribus auctos
non temere ulla vi convinci posse putabant.
fortunisque ideo longe praestare putabant,
quod mortis timor haud quemquam vexaret eorum,   1180
et simul in somnis quia multa et mira videbant
efficere et nullum capere ipsos inde laborem.
    Praeterea caeli rationes ordine certo
et varia annorum cernebant tempora verti
nec poterant quibus id fieret cognoscere causis.   1185
ergo perfugium sibi habebant omnia divis
tradere et illorum nutu facere omnia flecti.
in caeloque deum sedis et templa locarunt,
per caelum volvi quia nox et luna videtur,
luna dies et nox et noctis signa severa   1190
noctivagaeque faces caeli flammaeque volantes,
nubila sol imbres nix venti fulmina grando
et rapidi fremitus et murmura magna minarum.
    O genus infelix humanum, talia divis
cum tribuit facta atque iras adiunxit acerbas!   1195
quantos tum gemitus ipsi sibi, quantaque nobis
vulnera, quas lacrimas peperere minoribu' nostris!
nec pietas ullast velatum saepe videri
vertier ad lapidem atque omnis accedere ad aras
nec procumbere humi prostratum et pandere palmas   1200
ante deum delubra nec aras sanguine multo
spargere quadrupedum nec votis nectere vota,
sed mage pacata posse omnia mente tueri.
nam cum suspicimus magni caelestia mundi
templa super stellisque micantibus aethera fixum,   1205
et venit in mentem solis lunaeque viarum,
tunc aliis oppressa malis in pectora cura
illa quoque expergefactum caput erigere infit,
nequae forte deum nobis immensa potestas

1210 sit, vario motu quae candida sidera verset.
  temptat enim dubiam mentem rationis egestas,
  ecquaenam fuerit mundi genitalis origo,
  et simul ecquae sit finis, quoad moenia mundi
  solliciti motus hunc possint ferre laborem,
1215 an divinitus aeterna donata salute
  perpetuo possint aevi labentia tractu
  immensi validas aevi contemnere viris.
  praeterea cui non animus formidine divum
  contrahitur, cui non correpunt membra pavore,
1220 fulminis horribili cum plaga torrida tellus
  contremit et magnum percurrunt murmura caelum?
  non populi gentesque tremunt, regesque superbi
  corripiunt divum percussi membra timore,
  nequid ob admissum foede dictumve superbe
1225 poenarum grave sit solvendi tempus adultum?
  summa etiam cum vis violenti per mare venti
  induperatorem classis super aequora verrit
  cum validis pariter legionibus atque elephantis,
  non divum pacem votis adit ac prece quaesit
1230 ventorum pavidus paces animasque secundas,
  nequiquam, quoniam violento turbine saepe
  correptus nilo fertur minus ad vada leti?
  usque adeo res humanas vis abdita quaedam
  obterit et pulchros fascis saevasque securis
1235 proculcare ac ludibrio sibi habere videtur.
  denique sub pedibus tellus cum tota vacillat
  concussaeque cadunt urbes dubiaeque minantur,
  quid mirum si se temnunt mortalia saecla
  atque potestates magnas mirasque relinquunt
1240 in rebus viris divum, quae cuncta gubernent?

  The closing passage (ll. 1204–1240), especially the
phrase *vis abdita quaedam* (l. 1233), illustrates the inner
conflict in Lucretius. To Lucretius the philosopher the

nature of things is an open book. But Lucretius the
poet here describes with passion the feelings of fear
and mystery inspired by the great forces of nature.
Lucretius the philosopher believes that the sun and
moon are the size of not very large stones and are not
very distant.[1] Lucretius the poet describes the awe
that falls upon a man in the presence of the vastness
of the starry sky.[2] He writes with an intensity which
suggests not that he is merely trying to sympathize
from a distance with the doubts and fears of non-
Epicurean mankind, but that he is describing his own
feelings. He writes here in a tone very different from
that in which he sets down the orthodox Epicurean
theory about the size of the sun and moon.

The remainder of Book v deals with other aspects
of the progress of mankind. A chance forest-fire re-
vealed the possibility of smelting metals. The use of
bronze was first discovered, then the use of iron. The
use of iron initiated developments in various fields, of
which Lucretius deals with three: (1) the art of war-
fare, (2) clothing ("for by iron the loom is fashioned"),
(3) cultivation of the soil.

The art of music took its origin in the imitation of
songs of birds. Men later introduced elaborations of
their own; "nor yet for all that", adds Lucretius,
expressing a characteristic Epicurean sentiment,"do
they gain a whit greater enjoyment from the pleasure,
than the woodland race of earthborn men of old. For
what is here at hand, unless we have learnt anything
sweeter before, pleases us above all, and is thought to
excel, but for the most part the better thing found later
on destroys or changes our feeling for all the old things.
...And so the race of men toils fruitlessly and in vain

[1] See Passage 12.
[2] *Esp.* ll. 1204–1210; and cf. VI. 58 ff. (Passage 18).

for ever, and wastes its life in idle cares, because, we may be sure, it has not learned what are the limits of possession, nor at all how far true pleasure can increase." This is of importance to an understanding of the Epicurean view of the *value* of progress.

But it is the *process* by which progress has been achieved that has been Lucretius' chief concern throughout this part of his work, and it is his emphasis on the process that gives unity to what is otherwise (in its present state) a somewhat unmethodical account of man's development. The process is in every instance the same. Nothing has a divine origin: everything takes its origin from the operation of natural causes. Once nature has played her part in providing the start, man carries on the second part of the process summarized in the following lines (1452, 1453):

> usus et impigrae simul experientia mentis
> paulatim docuit pedetemptim progredientis.

"Practice and therewith the enterprise of the eager mind taught mankind little by little, as they went forward step by step." Nature and man's native wit alone, without any divine intervention, have raised man from the status of the beast to his present condition: that is the great truth which Lucretius is bent on inculcating at every stage in his account.

B (*f*) *Various celestial and terrestrial phenomena.* Book VI

Book VI is closely connected in subject with Book V, just as IV is closely connected with III, and II with I. In both V and VI Lucretius' purpose is to show that the phenomena of the world around us can all be explained by natural causes. Book V deals with phenomena obeying regular laws or exhibiting an apparently rational design (e.g. the motions of the heavenly bodies, and the development of mankind).

Such phenomena, because they obey regular laws, may lead men to a belief in a divine controlling power. Another class of phenomena, on the other hand, may startle the less rational of mankind into a belief in a divine power because of their apparently irregular or miraculous nature. It is this second class of phenomena, with which Lucretius deals in Book VI.[1]

After the prooemium the book naturally falls into two halves. At l. 50 Lucretius promises to explain things *quae fieri in terris caeloque tuentur* / *mortales*, and this gives us the two main sub-divisions of his subject. (1) (96–534) He deals with celestial phenomena: thunder, lightning (including the thunderbolt), waterspouts, clouds and rain. (2) (535–1286) He deals with a variety of topics connected with phenomena occurring on earth: earthquakes; why does the sea remain constant in size? the eruptions of Etna; the rise of the Nile; lakes that give out poisonous exhalations; curious springs; the magnet; pestilences, for example the plague at Athens described by Thucydides.

This book is a picture-gallery of scenes from nature. There are many examples of first-hand observation and acute inference, thus: "If you see some one far off cutting down a giant tree with double-edged axe, it comes to pass that you see the stroke before the blow resounds in your ear; even so we see the lightning too before we hear the thunder." In connection with clouds we find one of the few passages in classical literature that refer to mountain-climbing. In connection with the magnet we find the only passage in the *de R.N.* where Lucretius describes an actual experiment.[2]

Though the problems discussed seem to be set down almost at random, the method employed throughout

---

[1] Giuss., n. on Book VI *init*.
[2] The passages referred to are 167 ff., 459 ff., 906 ff.

the book remains constant. The problem must be reduced, wherever possible, to its simplest terms, i.e. to terms of atomic movement. This method is used with special ingenuity in connection with the magnet, and also in connection with the spring of Ammon, in the Libyan desert, which was supposed to be cold by day and warm by night.[1] Lucretius' constant return to the Atom gives some unity to a book which would otherwise be lacking in it.

The book closes with a piece of first-hand observation, originally made and recorded by Thucydides, of the plague at Athens.[2] Lucretius' account (1138–1286) is partly imitation, partly direct translation. There is no reason why the *de R.N.* should end with this account,[3] and there is little doubt that the poem as we have it is incomplete. One especially glaring omission is dealt with in the following section.

B (g) *The gods*

The gods, like all things else, are composed of material atoms. Their component atoms, like the atoms of the human soul, are finer than ordinary atoms, but are none the less material. Thus the nature of the gods is a subject which comes under the heading of Natura Rerum, Physical Science. We should therefore expect Lucretius to deal fully with this subject, as he has dealt with all other branches of physical science; and there are two passages which show that he did in fact

[1] 848 ff. If an Epicurean could have gone there armed with a thermometer, he might have discovered a simpler explanation.

[2] Thuc. II. 48 ff. "For I was myself attacked, and witnessed the sufferings of others."

[3] An ingenious explanation is offered by H. S. Davies, p. 38.

intend to do so. (1) In his exordium (Passage 1) he touches on (a) the terrors of religion and their effect, (b) the fear of death. Later he deals fully with (b) in Book III, but never with (a). (2) At v. 155 (Passage 14 below) he promises to "prove hereafter with copious argument" the Epicurean theory about the gods, but in the *de R.N.* as we have it his promise is never fulfilled. It is therefore reasonable to suppose that if he had completed his work he would have added a section on the nature of the gods and the ideal state of ἀταραξία in which they live.

There are, however, a number of scattered references to the subject throughout the *de R.N.*, from which some points in the Epicurean theory can be gathered. From passages 14–16 we learn the following: (1) The nature of the gods is *tenuis*: that is, they are composed of fine atoms. (2) They dwell outside the world, in the spaces between worlds (*intermundia* is the word used by Cicero in describing the Epicurean theory). (3) They live in a state of untroubled bliss. (4) They do not control nature and they have no concern whatever with the affairs of the world.[1]

14. v. 146–155

Illud item non est ut possis credere, sedis   146
esse deum sanctas in mundi partibus ullis.
tenvis enim natura deum longeque remota'
sensibus ab nostris animi vix mente videtur;
quae quoniam manuum tactum suffugit et ictum,   150
tactile nil nobis quod sit contingere debet.
tangere enim non quit quod tangi non licet ipsum.
quare etiam sedes quoque nostris sedibus esse
dissimiles debent, tenues de corpore eorum;
quae tibi posterius largo sermone probabo.   155

[1] Further passages enforcing this fourth point by various arguments are II. 177–181, V. 156–234, VI. 387–422.

15. III. 14-24

14   Nam simul ac ratio tua coepit vociferari
     naturam rerum, divina mente coorta,
     diffugiunt animi terrores, moenia mundi
     discedunt, totum video per inane geri res.
     apparet divum numen sedesque quietae
     quas neque concutiunt venti nec nubila nimbis
20   aspergunt neque nix acri concreta pruina
     cana cadens violat semperque innubilus aether
     integit, et large diffuso lumine ridet.
     omnia suppeditat porro natura neque ulla
24   res animi pacem delibat tempore in ullo.

16. II. 1090-1104

1090 Quae bene cognita si teneas, natura videtur
      libera continuo dominis privata superbis
      ipsa sua per se sponte omnia dis agere expers.
      nam pro sancta deum tranquilla pectora pace
      quae placidum degunt aevum vitamque serenam,
1095 quis regere immensi summam, quis habere profundi
      indu manu validas potis est moderanter habenas,
      quis pariter caelos omnis convertere et omnis
      ignibus aetheriis terras suffire feraces,
      omnibus inve locis esse omni tempore praesto,
1100 nubibus ut tenebras faciat caelique serena
      concutiat sonitu, tum fulmina mittat et aedes
      saepe suas disturbet et in deserta recedens
      saeviat exercens telum quod saepe nocentis
1104 praeterit exanimatque indignos inque merentis?

     In this last passage Lucretius runs two quite distinct
arguments together. The gods do not control nature
because (a) we cannot conceive of the existence of a
being powerful enough, and ubiquitous enough, to

control all the forces of nature throughout the number-less worlds, (b) some of the forces of nature, e.g. the thunderbolt, operate in a notoriously indiscriminate way. (The second argument is developed at greater length, again in connection with thunder, at VI. 387–422.)

Lucretius shows here an imaginative realization of the staggering greatness of natural forces such as is found in Hebrew literature.

> Where wast thou when I laid the foundations of the earth? declare, if thou hast understanding.
> Who hath laid the measures thereof, if thou knowest? or who hath stretched the line upon it?
> Whereupon are the foundations thereof fastened? or who laid the corner stone thereof;
> When the morning stars sang together, and all the sons of God shouted for joy? [1]

It is an attitude of mind more usually connected with some kind of pantheism than with the complete materialism of Epicurus. We see here yet another example of the internal struggle in Lucretius between poet and scientist: the imaginative description of the grandeur of the universe sorts ill with the truth that it is meant to enforce, namely that all this is caused only by the blind whirl of atoms.

Two further points in the Epicurean teaching about the nature of the gods may be gathered from Lucretius' scattered references. (1) The gods are human in form, as the nature of their Idols proves.[2] (2) "It must needs be that all the nature of the gods enjoys *life everlasting* in perfect peace."[3] But, since the gods are composed of material atoms, how can they enjoy *aevum immortale*? Various ingenious explanations of this difficulty have

---

[1] Job xxxviii. 4 ff. and cf. the whole of chs. xxxvii–xli.
[2] v. 1169 ff. (Passage 13).   [3] II. 646, 647.

been offered: we are told that the gods, like all other
compound bodies,[1] remain constant only in form, not
in matter; the actual atoms which compose them are
continually departing and fresh atoms streaming in.
But no other compound body remains immortal; and
there is no doubt that we have here an inconsistency
in the system which cannot be explained away in
atomic terms. The reason for the inconsistency will
become clear if we consider the wider question, Why
did such a thorough-going materialist as Epicurus
suppose that the gods existed at all?

The answer is two-fold:

(1) Their existence is proved by the existence of
Idols of gods which appear to men in visions. These
Idols must be due to a physical cause, and they remain
too constant in appearance to be ascribed to the chance
spontaneous formation of Idols in the air.

(2) The second reason lies outside the confines of
materialist reasoning. The teaching of Epicurus about
the gods had a moral purpose. In the life of the gods
Epicurus wished to see his ideal of happiness realized.
The Epicurean gods were in fact perfect Epicureans—
perfect exemplars of a state of $\dot{a}\tau a\rho a\xi\dot{i}a$, "peace of
mind". Reason, writes Lucretius, can overcome human
weakness to such an extent "that nothing hinders us
from living a life *worthy of the gods.*"[2] Now the two
great enemies to the perfect state of bliss are fear of
the gods and fear of death. The gods are obviously
exempt from the first; but to make them entirely
exempt from the second it is necessary to pre-suppose
not merely that they are long-lived but that they are
immortal. Hence arose the inconsistency which we
have noted above.

This summarizes the teaching of Epicurus about the

[1] See p. 38.   [2] III. 322.

existence and the nature of the gods—a subject with which Lucretius intended but failed to deal fully. The question of man's proper attitude towards the gods will come under the third and last main heading of our analysis of Epicureanism, namely, under Ethics.

C. Ethics

Epicurus was primarily a moral teacher, not a natural scientist. Lucretius writes primarily as a natural scientist and only now and then as a moral teacher (although of course he too looks on natural science as the handmaid of morals). In the following account, therefore, of the Epicurean system of ethics, we can fill in only part of the picture with material drawn directly from Lucretius, and the rest of the picture has to be completed from other sources.

Before any system of ethics can be constructed, one preliminary question has to be answered. Does man possess free-will? If the answer is "No", it is clearly useless to proceed any further. It is not easy for a completely materialist philosophy such as that of Epicurus to answer anything but "No", for if everything is matter then everything must obey the remorseless laws of cause and effect which we see operating in the world of matter around us. We have already seen how Epicurus got round the difficulty by his assumption of the "atomic swerve" (Passage 7).

C 1 PLEASURE

Once it has been established that mankind has the power of choice, the fundamental question of any ethical enquiry can be put: What is the ultimate goal of human conduct? In order to answer this Epicurus does not presuppose any abstract ideal, e.g. God or the good of Humanity, but simply applies the primary law of Canonic, just as he applied it in the sphere of Natural Science. Our senses are infallible. Our senses tell us that every man seeks pleasure and avoids pain. "All living creatures as soon as they are born take delight in pleasure, but resist pain by a natural impulse apart from reason."[1] Therefore Pleasure is the ultimate goal, and man's primary duty is to aim at Pleasure.[2]

But our senses also tell us that Pleasure often breeds Pain. Therefore present Pleasure must sometimes be sacrificed in order to avoid future Pain, and present Pain must sometimes be incurred with a view to greater future Pleasure. It is clear then that in order to lead the good life the Epicurean must be able to calculate "amounts" of Pleasure and Pain, so that he may enjoy the maximum of Pleasure and the minimum of Pain. Are there any general rules which may guide him in doing this?

Epicurus' answer is that there are two kinds of Pleasure, active and passive.[3] Active pleasure is the pleasure we experience in the actual satisfying of a desire; passive pleasure the conscious enjoyment of a state of equilibrium in which no desires are felt. For instance: I am thirsty and drink a pint of beer; while I am drinking I enjoy active pleasure; when I have finished I enjoy passive pleasure in the consciousness of thirst satisfied. Now although active pleasure may be more acute than passive pleasure it is necessarily accompanied by a desire (=Pain) which it removes, and which through force of habit it is likely to bring

---

[1] Epicurus quoted by Diogenes Laertius, x. 137.

[2] Our criterion of what is pleasant and what painful is "feeling" ($\pi\acute{a}\theta$os), which according to Epicurus is as infallible in deciding this question as is "sensation" ($a\check{i}\sigma\theta\eta\sigma\iota s$) in *its* proper sphere of activity.

[3] $\mathring{\eta}$ $\mathring{\epsilon}\nu$ $\kappa\iota\nu\mathring{\eta}\sigma\epsilon\iota$ ($\mathring{\eta}\delta o\nu\mathring{\eta}$), and $\mathring{\eta}$ $\kappa\alpha\tau\alpha\sigma\tau\eta\mu\alpha\tau\iota\kappa\mathring{\eta}$.

into being again. It is therefore not pure pleasure. The only pure pleasure is passive pleasure, in which there is no desire and therefore no Pain, the state described by Epicurus in the word ἀταραξία. If we have a desire it is good to satisfy it, but it is better still to have no desire. The good life then is the life which embraces the maximum of passive pleasure, of conscious enjoyment of a state of equilibrium.

Thus the Epicurean conception of Pleasure in its highest form is very different from what we normally mean by the word pleasure and from what Greeks normally meant by the word ἡδονή. In making ἡδονή the key-word of his system of ethics Epicurus perhaps reveals an unphilosophical desire to *épater les bourgeois*, or at least a desire to present his teaching in an arresting way. Partly as a result of this, his teaching has come in for a great deal of criticism, from his day to the present, which it might have avoided altogether; and the word Epicurean, in its modern meaning of "self-indulgent", has departed far from its proper meaning.

In the following passage Lucretius vehemently declares that the only pleasure to be sought is freedom from pain and fear. "Nature cries aloud for nothing else but that pain may be kept far sundered from the body, and that, withdrawn from care and fear, she may enjoy in mind the sense of pleasure." As an example of the enjoyment of such pleasure Lucretius describes a simple picnic.—Epicurus loved the country with a love that was unusual in his day, and he was the first to establish a large garden within the city of Athens—a garden that was destined to be famous.

17. II. 1–33

Suave, mari magno turbantibus aequora ventis,   1
e terra magnum alterius spectare laborem;
non quia vexari quemquamst iucunda voluptas,

sed quibus ipse malis careas quia cernere suave est.
5 suave etiam belli certamina magna tueri
per campos instructa tua sine parte pericli.
sed nil dulcius est, bene quam munita tenere
edita doctrina sapientum templa serena,
despicere unde queas alios passimque videre
10 errare atque viam palantis quaerere vitae,
certare ingenio, contendere nobilitate,
noctes atque dies niti praestante labore
ad summas emergere opes rerumque potiri.
o miseras hominum mentis, o pectora caeca!
15 qualibus in tenebris vitae quantisque periclis
degitur hoc aevi quodcumquest! nonne videre
nil aliud sibi naturam latrare, nisi utqui
corpore seiunctus dolor absit, mente fruatur
iucundo sensu cura semota metuque?
20 ergo corpoream ad naturam pauca videmus
esse opus omnino, quae demant cumque dolorem,
delicias quoque uti multas substernere possint.
gratius interdum neque natura ipsa requirit,
si non aurea sunt iuvenum simulacra per aedes
25 lampadas igniferas manibus retinentia dextris,
lumina nocturnis epulis ut suppeditentur,
nec domus argento fulget auroque renidet
nec citharae reboant laqueata aurataque templa,
cum tamen inter se prostrati in gramine molli
30 propter aquae rivum sub ramis arboris altae
non magnis opibus iucunde corpora curant,
praesertim cum tempestas arridet et anni
tempora conspergunt viridantis floribus herbas.

The enjoyment of the highest form of Pleasure, tranquillity of mind, is, according to Epicurus, rendered difficult for the mass of mankind by two main sources of disturbance, fear of the gods and fear of death. It was

in order to destroy these fears that Epicurus studied
and taught Natural Science, and this was also Lucretius'
main purpose, as we saw in Passage 1, in writing the
de R.N. At this point it is relevant to consider in more
detail the Epicurean teaching about the attitude which
the wise man will take towards, first, the gods, and
second, death.

C 1 (a) *Freedom from fear of the gods*

The Epicurean theory about the nature of the gods has
already been discussed. We have also seen the reasons
which Epicurus assigned for the origin of religion,
namely, visions of the gods and ignorance of the cause
of celestial phenomena.[1] The question of the wise man's
attitude towards the gods remains to be discussed.
Epicurus' teaching on this subject is surprising. The
wise man will not merely set his mind at rest by rooting
out the fear of the gods; but he will become more truly
religious than the orthodox believer. He will be a
worshipper of the gods, though his worship will not
consist of prayers for divine interference in the world,
which is impossible. His worship will consist rather
of contemplating and "drinking in" the ideal Epicurean
state of tranquillity that is realized in the life of the
gods.[2] Thus it is fair to say that Epicurus was responsible for the noblest interpretation that was ever
put on the popular religion of the Greco-Roman world.

Lucretius in the following passage, which comes
strangely from the pen of so vehement a materialist,
describes the nature of true Epicurean worship.

18. VI. 58–79

Nam bene qui didicere deos securum agere aevum, 58
si tamen interea mirantur qua ratione

[1] v. 1161–1240 (Passage 13).
[2] See B (g), pp. 78–83.

60 quaeque geri possint, praesertim rebus in illis
quae supera caput aetheriis cernuntur in oris,
rursus in antiquas referuntur religiones
et dominos acris adsciscunt, omnia posse
quos miseri credunt, ignari quid queat esse,
65 quid nequeat, finita potestas denique cuique
quanam sit ratione atque alte terminus haerens;
quo magis errantes caeca ratione feruntur.
quae nisi respuis ex animo longeque remittis
dis indigna putare alienaque pacis eorum,
70 delibata deum per te tibi numina sancta
saepe oberunt; non quo violari summa deum vis
possit, ut ex ira poenas petere imbibat acris,
sed quia tute tibi placida cum pace quietos
constitues magnos irarum volvere fluctus,
75 nec delubra deum placido cum pectore adibis,
nec de corpore quae sancto simulacra feruntur
in mentis hominum divinae nuntia formae,
suscipere haec animi tranquilla pace valebis.
79 inde videre licet qualis iam vita sequatur.

C 1 (b) *Freedom from fear of death*

Towards the end of Book III, after pouring out a series
of twenty-eight proofs of the mortality of the soul,
Lucretius launches forth into a denunciation of the folly
of the fear of death.[1] In this passage, which is the
climax of the *de R.N.*, Lucretius leaves Natural Science
for the time being and enters the field of Ethics.

How far does his denunciation carry conviction?
Before attempting to answer this question we may state
as a generalization that there are two kinds of fear of
death. First, there is the irrational fear of suffering in

---

[1] For the context see p. 48.

store after death. This fear might be taken as an illustration of *tantum religio potuit suadere malorum*. Lucretius no doubt knew of the tortures of the damned which were promised by Etruscan religion, and this connection between religion and hell-fire has been steadily maintained till fairly recent days.[1] Second, there is the rational fear of death—whether our own death or that of our friends—as the end of human ties and of all the other experiences and joys of life.

Let us now consider Lucretius' "Consolation" and see how far he was successful in attacking either or both of these fears. The next passage (III. 830–977) may be summarized as follows:

(830–893) We shall not be conscious of anything when once we are dead (*mortalem vitam mors cum immortalis ademit*), any more than we are now conscious of things which occurred before we were alive. Anyone who professes to believe this, and yet laments because his body may be committed to flames or torn by beasts, shows that he is still under the domination of irrational feeling, of some *caecus stimulus* in his own heart.— Lucretius, dealing here with a simple form of the first fear, has things all his own way.

(894–930) Death, men say, means an end to the affections and the joys of life. But it also means an end to the longing for these things: there is therefore no cause to grieve either for our own death or for the deaths of our friends. Men also say, "Eat drink and be merry, for to-morrow we die." But why cram life with pleasures as though it were preparatory to an existence full of pain? In death we shall not miss life and its sensations any more than in sleep.—Lucretius here attempts to deal with the second kind of fear of death. How far he is successful is a matter for each reader's own judgement, but we may well feel that in

---

[1] On the question of Greco-Roman belief in an after-life see Sikes pp. 124 ff. and refs. there.

ll. 894–903 his heart is at war with his head and that
his heart is really victorious.[1] Lucretius is not alone
in finding Reason a powerless weapon in dealing with
this problem.

(931–977) Lucretius continues his attack on the
second kind of fear of death. If life has been pleasant,
retire satisfied, *ut plenus vitae conviva*. If unpleasant,
why grieve to end it? The endless chain of life-death-
life must continue. "There is need of matter for the
growth of the generations to come." We enter into
possession of life not as owners of the freehold but
only as tenants, not *mancipio* but *usu*.—Here Lucretius
offers the best consolation that Reason can give: view
life and death from a universal standpoint, and it is
merely ignorant conceit if we think that our individual
death is of the least importance.

19. III. 830–977

830   Nil igitur mors est ad nos neque pertinet hilum,
      quandoquidem natura animi mortalis habetur.
      et velut anteacto nil tempore sensimus aegri,
      ad confligendum venientibus undique Poenis,
      omnia cum belli trepido concussa tumultu
835   horrida contremuere sub altis aetheris oris,
      in dubioque fuere utrorum ad regna cadendum
      omnibus humanis esset terraque marique,
      sic, ubi non erimus, cum corporis atque animai
      discidium fuerit quibus e sumus uniter apti,
840   scilicet haud nobis quicquam, qui non erimus tum,
      accidere omnino poterit sensumque movere,
      non si terra mari miscebitur et mare caelo.
      et si iam nostro sentit de corpore postquam
      distractast animi natura animaeque potestas,
845   nil tamen est ad nos qui comptu coniugioque

                    [1] See Intro. pp. xviii ff.

corporis atque animae consistimus uniter apti.
nec, si materiem nostram collegerit aetas
post obitum rursumque redegerit ut sita nunc est
atque iterum nobis fuerint data lumina vitae,
pertineat quicquam tamen ad nos id quoque factum,   850
interrupta semel cum sit repetentia nostri.
et nunc nil ad nos de nobis attinet, ante
qui fuimus, nil iam de illis nos adficit angor.
nam cum respicias immensi temporis omne
praeteritum spatium, tum motus materiai   855
multimodis quam sint, facile hoc accredere possis,
semina saepe in eodem, ut nunc sunt, ordine posta
haec eadem, quibus e nunc nos sumus, ante fuisse.
nec memori tamen id quimus reprehendere mente;
inter enim iectast vitai pausa vageque   860
deerrarunt passim motus ab sensibus omnes.
debet enim, misere si forte aegreque futurumst,
ipse quoque esse in eo tum tempore, cui male possit
accidere. id quoniam mors eximit, esseque probet
illum cui possint incommoda conciliari,   865
scire licet nobis nil esse in morte timendum
nec miserum fieri qui non est posse neque hilum
differre an nullo fuerit iam tempore natus,
mortalem vitam mors cum immortalis ademit.
    Proinde ubi se videas hominem indignarier ipsum,   870
post mortem fore ut aut putescat corpore posto
aut flammis interfiat malisve ferarum,
scire licet non sincerum sonere atque subesse
caecum aliquem cordi stimulum, quamvis neget ipse
credere se quemquam sibi sensum in morte futurum. 875
non, ut opinor, enim dat quod promittit et unde,
nec radicitus e vita se tollit et eicit,
sed facit esse sui quiddam super inscius ipse.
vivus enim sibi cum proponit quisque futurum,

880 corpus uti volucres lacerent in morte feraeque,
ipse sui miseret; neque enim se dividit illim
nec removet satis a proiecto corpore et illum
se fingit sensuque suo contaminat adstans.
hinc indignatur se mortalem esse creatum
885 nec videt in vera nullum fore morte alium se
qui possit vivus sibi se lugere peremptum
stansque iacentem se lacerari urive dolere.
nam si in morte malumst malis morsuque ferarum
tractari, non invenio qui non sit acerbum
890 ignibus impositum calidis torrescere flammis
aut in melle situm suffocari atque rigere
frigore, cum summo gelidi cubat aequore saxi,
urgerive superne obtritum pondere terrae.
"Iam iam non domus accipiet te laeta, neque uxor
895 optima nec dulces occurrent oscula nati
praeripere et tacita pectus dulcedine tangent.
non poteris factis florentibus esse, tuisque
praesidium. misero misere" aiunt "omnia ademit
una dies infesta tibi tot praemia vitae."
900 illud in his rebus non addunt "nec tibi earum
iam desiderium rerum super insidet una."
quod bene si videant animo dictisque sequantur,
dissoluant animi magno se angore metuque.
"tu quidem ut es leto sopitus, sic eris aevi
905 quod superest cunctis privatu' doloribus aegris.
at nos horrifico cinefactum te prope busto
insatiabiliter deflevimus, aeternumque
nulla dies nobis maerorem e pectore demet."
illud ab hoc igitur quaerendum est, quid sit amari
910 tanto opere, ad somnum si res redit atque quietem,
cur quisquam aeterno possit tabescere luctu.
    Hoc etiam faciunt ubi discubuere tenentque
pocula saepe homines et inumbrant ora coronis,

ex animo ut dicant "brevis hic est fructus homullis;
iam fuerit neque post umquam revocare licebit."   915
tamquam in morte mali cum primis hoc sit eorum,
quod sitis exurat miseros atque arida torrat,
aut aliae cuius desiderium insideat rei.
nec sibi enim quisquam tum se vitamque requirit,
cum pariter mens et corpus sopita quiescunt.   920
nam licet aeternum per nos sic esse soporem,
nec desiderium nostri nos adficit ullum.
et tamen haudquaquam nostros tunc illa per artus
longe ab sensiferis primordia motibus errant,
cum correptus homo ex somno se colligit ipse.   925
multo igitur mortem minus ad nos esse putandumst,
si minus esse potest quam quod nil esse videmus;
maior enim turba et disiectus materiai
consequitur leto nec quisquam expergitus exstat,
frigida quem semel est vitai pausa secuta.   930
  Denique si vocem rerum natura repente
mittat et hoc alicui nostrum sic increpet ipsa
"quid tibi tanto operest, mortalis, quod nimis aegris
luctibus indulges? quid mortem congemis ac fles?
nam si grata fuit tibi vita anteacta priorque   935
et non omnia pertusum congesta quasi in vas
commoda perfluxere atque ingrata interiere,
cur non ut plenus vitae conviva recedis
aequo animoque capis securam, stulte, quietem?
sin ea quae fructus cumque es periere profusa   940
vitaque in offensast, cur amplius addere quaeris,
rursum quod pereat male et ingratum occidat omne,
non potius vitae finem facis atque laboris?
nam tibi praeterea quod machiner inveniamque,
quod placeat, nil est: eadem sunt omnia semper.   945
si tibi non annis corpus iam marcet et artus
confecti languent, eadem tamen omnia restant,

omnia si pergas vivendo vincere saecla,
atque etiam potius, si numquam sis moriturus",
950 quid respondemus, nisi iustam intendere litem
naturam et veram verbis exponere causam?
grandior hic vero si iam seniorque queratur
atque obitum lamentetur miser amplius aequo,
non merito inclamet magis et voce increpet acri?
955 "aufer abhinc lacrimas, balatro, et compesce querelas.
omnia perfunctus vitai praemia marces.
sed quia semper aves quod abest, praesentia temnis,
imperfecta tibi elapsast ingrataque vita
et nec opinanti mors ad caput adstitit ante
960 quam satur ac plenus possis discedere rerum.
nunc aliena tua tamen aetate omnia mitte
aequo animoque agedum gnatis concede: necessest."
iure, ut opinor, agat, iure increpet inciletque.
cedit enim rerum novitate extrusa vetustas
965 semper, et ex aliis aliud reparare necessest:
nec quisquam in barathrum nec Tartara deditur atra.
materies opus est ut crescant postera saecla;
quae tamen omnia te vita perfuncta sequentur;
nec minus ergo ante haec quam tu cecidere, cadentque.
970 sic alid ex alio numquam desistet oriri
vitaque mancipio nulli datur, omnibus usu.
respice item quam nil ad nos anteacta vetustas
temporis aeterni fuerit, quam nascimur ante.
hoc igitur speculum nobis natura futuri
975 temporis exponit post mortem denique nostram.
numquid ibi horribile apparet, num triste videtur
quicquam, non omni somno securius exstat?

The remainder of Lucretius' denunciation of the fear
of death may be summarized as follows:

(978–1023) He returns to the first kind of fear of
death. Tales of torment in an after-life are merely

allegories of the miseries of this life: Sisyphus, for instance, allegorizes the ambitious and unsuccessful aspirant for the honours of public life, and so on. "It is here on earth that the life of fools becomes a Hell" (l. 1023).

(1024–1094) Lucretius concludes in a tone of scornful and satirical admonition. The great and good men of the past have died: why not *you*, "whose life is well-nigh dead while you still live"? If men only knew the cause of their restless craving for pleasure (namely sub-conscious fear of death), they would abandon all else in order to study the nature of things and rid themselves of their fear. Finally, it is useless to crave for longer life: however long we live, there is no new pleasure in store for us; however long we live, the period of death will still be infinite.

Thus we see that Lucretius attacks the fear of death on both fronts. On one front, where the forces of religion were arrayed against him, he has little difficulty in routing the enemy. On the other front, where his own feelings were to some extent fighting on the other side, he can hardly be said to be victorious; but his poetry is a magnificent record of a conflict which is common to all humanity.

C 2 *Virtue*

In the Epicurean system there is no place for Virtue, if, along with orthodox moralists, we consider Virtue as the *end* of action. Virtue to the Epicurean cannot be an end, though it may be a useful means of attaining the true end, Pleasure. "I spit upon the honourable", wrote Epicurus, "and upon those who vainly admire it, when it does not produce any pleasure."[1] How far then in practice does the life of the Epicurean differ

---

[1] B. Epic. fr. 79.

from the life of orthodox virtue? In order to answer this it will be convenient to take some of the traditional virtues separately and consider them as examples.

The "self-regarding" virtues, e.g. temperance and courage, can be dealt with very shortly. The Epicurean definition of Pleasure implies that temperance must be practised by the Epicurean: he will avoid, as far as he may, "active pleasure" and its accompanying desire or pain. The Epicurean will also be courageous, for courage is the choosing of pains, as one ancient writer sums it up, "in order to avoid greater pains"; moreover courage will come easily and naturally to an Epicurean, since he knows the folly of the fear of death.

The "other-regarding" virtues raise more interesting problems. These, and the general question of the Epicurean's relations with his fellow-men, will be considered under four headings.

C 2 (a) *Justice*

Justice is in itself an evil, injustice a good, since the ideal of the individual is to have unfettered freedom of choice and to be a law unto himself. The observance of justice is merely a means to freedom from fear of other men; and, historically speaking, justice came into being, as we have seen, with the voluntarily formed Social Contract.[1] The question obviously arising out of this is put by Epicurus himself in the following words: "Will the wise man do things that the laws forbid, if he knows that he will not be found out?" And he answers the question with a human lack of certainty: "A simple answer is not easy to find."[2] But his answer is elsewhere made clear enough. "Though he be unnoticed of the race of gods and men,

[1] v. 1011–1027, 1136–1160 (Passage 13).
[2] B. Epic. fr. 2.

yet he must needs mistrust that his secret will be kept
for ever."[1] However secretive we may be, we cannot
be altogether free of the fear of discovery: but fear
impairs our tranquillity of mind: therefore we must
avoid the injustice which causes the fear. Thus in
practice the Epicurean and the orthodox just man
behave in the same way, but the reasons they would
give for their behaviour are different.

The harsh frankness of the Epicurean view is modified by the following passage in the *de R.N.*, which is
one of the most profound passages in the whole work.
Injustice, Lucretius writes, is "fostered not least by
fear of death", which drives men to seek escape and
forgetfulness in feverish self-seeking activity. It is clear
that this introduces a far higher conception into the
Epicurean theory of justice. The wise man, being
exempt from the fear of death, is also exempt from one
of the main motives to transgression of justice. Justice,
like courage, comes naturally to the Epicurean.

20. III. 59–93

Denique avarities et honorum caeca cupido   59
quae miseros homines cogunt transcendere finis
iuris et interdum socios scelerum atque ministros
noctes atque dies niti praestante labore
ad summas emergere opes, haec vulnera vitae
non minimam partem mortis formidine aluntur.
turpis enim ferme contemptus et acris egestas   65
semota ab dulci vita stabilique videtur
et quasi iam leti portas cunctarier ante;
unde homines dum se falso terrore coacti
effugisse volunt longe longeque remosse,
sanguine civili rem conflant divitiasque   70
conduplicant avidi, caedem caede accumulantes;

---

[1] v. 1156–1157 (Passage 13), and cf. III. 1011–1023.

crudeles gaudent in tristi funere fratris
et consanguineum mensas odere timentque.
consimili ratione ab eodem saepe timore
75 macerat invidia ante oculos illum esse potentem,
illum aspectari, claro qui incedit honore,
ipsi se in tenebris volvi caenoque queruntur.
intereunt partim statuarum et nominis ergo.
et saepe usque adeo, mortis formidine, vitae
80 percipit humanos odium lucisque videndae,
ut sibi consciscant maerenti pectore letum
obliti fontem curarum hunc esse timorem,
hunc vexare pudorem, hunc vincula amicitiai
rumpere et e summa pietatem evertere sede.
85 nam iam saepe homines patriam carosque parentis
prodiderunt, vitare Acherusia templa petentes.
nam veluti pueri trepidant atque omnia caecis
in tenebris metuunt, sic nos in luce timemus
interdum, nilo quae sunt metuenda magis quam
90 quae pueri in tenebris pavitant finguntque futura.
hunc igitur terrorem animi tenebrasque necessest
non radii solis neque lucida tela diei
discutiant, sed naturae species ratioque.

This passage is remarkably interesting in itself, apart
from its connection with Epicurean ethics. The conception which it embodies has a strikingly modern ring.
Avarice, ambition, civil war, murder, and finally even
suicide—all of which abounded in the Rome of the
first century B.C.—are all diagnosed as being caused not
least by fear of death. Lucretius means this not in the
crude sense that we kill others because if we do not
they will kill us; but in the much profounder sense that
our fear of death and our desire *to escape* from the
thought of that fear drive us to every kind of restless
activity. Sometimes the desire to escape from the fear

of death is so strong that it drives men to escape it in death itself. Lucretius is here putting forward a curiously modern view of the nature of crime, namely that it results from disease of the mind, and therefore, by implication, is to be prevented not by punishment but by psychological treatment or, as Lucretius would put it, by study of the "nature of things".

Whether the much-used phrase "the restlessness of the modern generation" applies to one generation more than another it is difficult to say, but Lucretius carries conviction in his suggestion that the restlessness of every generation is largely attributable to unvoiced fear, whether it be fear of death or any of the rest of our fears, of all of which fear of death is no doubt the first begetter. All our *vulnera vitae*, amongst which we may include far more than the actual crimes that Lucretius enumerates, *non minimam partem mortis formidine aluntur*.[1]

C 2 (b) *Public life*

In his teaching on this subject Epicurus reveals with special clearness the historical circumstances which conditioned his whole system, namely the decay of the independent city-state and with it the decay of the sense of man's responsibilities as a citizen. If a man enters public life he exposes himself to many things likely to disturb his tranquillity of mind: the temptation to be ambitious and to envy his superiors, the fear of attack from his envious inferiors. The wise man therefore will avoid public life altogether. We have already come across the passage where Lucretius expresses this doctrine:[2]

> ...ut satius multo iam sit parere quietum
> quam regere imperio res velle et regna tenere.

[1] The same thought is present in the well-known passage about the vanity of change of residence, III. 1053–1075.

[2] v. 1120–1135 (Passage 13).

Two Greek words summed up the teaching of Epicurus on this subject: λάθε βιώσας, "live unnoticed".

C 2 (c) Love

In passionate love Epicurus saw the clearest example of the vicious circle created by "active pleasure": painful desire, satisfaction of it, recrudescence of the desire, and so on. The wise man therefore will entirely shun love. He may find it necessary to indulge in casual physical satisfaction of his lust, but he will at all costs avoid any entanglement of his affections; for if his affections become centred upon one object, his tranquillity of mind is at the mercy of another. Lucretius sets forth this cold doctrine with characteristic Epicurean frankness, Book IV, ll. 1058–1072.

C 2 (d) Friendship

Epicurus rejects passionate love, but his attitude to friendship is very different. In his own words, "Of all the things which wisdom acquires to produce the blessedness of the complete life, far the greatest is the possession of friendship."[1]

Friendship, to the Epicurean, is necessarily founded on self-interest: it is an unwritten compact for mutual protection and advantage. But from this unpromising root springs something that far transcends its origin, something that includes "genuine trust and unselfishness and even self-sacrifice".[2] In his views (and in his practice) of friendship Epicurus followed perhaps his human feelings rather than strict logic: certainly it is hard to justify on logical grounds his exalted view of friendship, unless we assume an un-Epicurean altruistic

[1] B. Epic. p. 100.
[2] B. p. 517, where a fuller account of Epicurean friendship may be found.

instinct to be present in man. Epicurus was famous in
antiquity for his friendships, and he was traditionally
pictured as the gentle philosopher of the Garden, surrounded by his circle of friends. In the Epicurean
doctrine of friendship we see the impress of Epicurus'
own personality rather than the result of impersonal
reasoning. In spite of this, or rather, perhaps, because
of this, he arrived at one of the most profound truths
in his whole system.

Whether Lucretius followed his master's example
we do not know. We may guess from his work that he
was too sombre and passionate to have been a man of
many friends. He does not anywhere expatiate on the
value of friendship. But the following passage has the
true Epicurean ring. Addressing Memmius, Lucretius
says that it is "the looked-for pleasure of your sweet
friendship" that is the motive force behind all the toil
which went to the composition of the *de R.N.*

21. I. 136–145

Nec me animi fallit Graiorum obscura reperta   136
difficile inlustrare Latinis versibus esse,
multa novis verbis praesertim cum sit agendum
propter egestatem linguae et rerum novitatem;
sed tua me virtus tamen et sperata voluptas   140
suavis amicitiae quemvis efferre laborem
suadet et inducit noctes vigilare serenas
quaerentem dictis quibus et quo carmine demum
clara tuae possim praepandere lumina menti,
res quibus occultas penitus convisere possis.   145

C 3 CONCLUSION

The merits of the *de R.N.* are not dependent on the value of Epicureanism, and it would therefore be out of place to attempt here an evaluation of Epicurus' moral teaching. But in conclusion a few general criticisms of it will be suggested.

The great merit of the Pleasure theory, in practice, is its flexibility and the allowances it makes for man's tendency to behave like a human being rather than like a philosopher's dummy. Epicurus recognizes that human instincts should be controlled, not repressed. Although, for instance, he was an enemy of the orthodox religion of his day, he recognizes that the religious instinct exists in human nature, and in his teaching about worship he suggests a reasonable and convenient outlet for it. Again, although he does not look on "active pleasure" as the highest form of Pleasure, he recognizes that within moderation it is both necessary and desirable. The doctrine that the highest form of Pleasure is tranquillity of mind does not make Epicureanism a way of life which finds its highest expression in asceticism, any more than the doctrine that Pleasure is the end of all action makes it the gospel of self-indulgence. The true position of Epicurus is clearly seen if we compare his teaching with that of two contemporary schools, the Stoics and the Cyrenaics. It is not unfair to say that Stoicism offered a way of life to the class of people—common enough at Rome and in England, perhaps less common in Greece—who enjoy *not* doing what they want to do. At the other extreme Cyrenaicism appealed to those who abandon themselves to the pleasure of the moment at the expense of life as a whole. The Epicurean occupies an intermediate position: he is not afraid to enjoy doing what he wants to do, but yet he has an eye to his life as a whole and not merely to the immediate present. He thus escapes the self-righteousness of the Stoic and the instability of the Cyrenaic. One chooses Epicureans, rather than Stoics or Cyrenaics, for one's friends; and this is a sufficient comment on the relative value of Epicurus' moral teaching. It is significant that friendship played so large a part both in the life and in the teaching of Epicurus.

At the same time there are two great deficiencies in Epicurus' theory of Pleasure. (1) The whole theory is founded on the supposition that man can be viewed as an individual completely separate from his fellows, that in considering the state of our feeling (i.e. Pleasure or Pain) we need take no account of the feelings of those around us. But this is manifestly not so, and Epicurus sought always to base his system not on what ought to be but on what is. For instance, as Guyau points out,[1] "Even the most self-centred pleasures, such as the pleasure of eating or of drinking, only acquire their full charm when we share them with another." Whether we like it or not, we cannot maintain that our feelings of Pleasure or Pain are entirely independent of those of others. It is a fact that man takes pleasure in altruism (whether altruism be finally analysable into self-interest or not is a question that does not affect the fact that altruism is pleasurable). Now Epicurus allows some outlet for the instinct of altruism in his teaching about friendship, but there is no reason why we should limit our pleasure in altruism to activity within the comparatively narrow bounds of friendship. "Morality", writes J. S. Mill, "consists in conscientious shrinking from the violation of moral rules; and the basis of this conscientious sentiment is the social feelings of mankind; the desire to be in unity with our fellow-creatures, which is already a

[1] *La Morale d'Épicure*, p. 283: the most interesting study of the subject.

powerful principle in human nature, and happily one of those which tend to become stronger from the influences of advancing civilization." We must realize the interdependence of human beings before we can arrive at a proper conception of the life of maximum Pleasure. The realization of this led to the modern doctrine of Utilitarianism, which adopted as its criterion not the Pleasure of the individual but "the greatest possible happiness of the greatest possible number". The enormous influence exerted by Utilitarianism on the modern world testifies both to the vitality inherent in Epicureanism, on which Utilitarianism is based, and to the magnitude of Epicurus' error in not allowing for the instinct of altruism.

(2) Epicurus' definition of the highest form of Pleasure as something static, as a state of bodily and mental equilibrium, is a definition which often seems attractive in a troublous and uncertain world, but it is a definition which men will certainly reject at times when their vitality is highest and they are "at their best". As we have seen above, the moral teaching of Epicurus is too flexible to be convicted of inculcating asceticism, but its tendency is certainly to err on the side of timidity. An Epicurean is not an ascetic, but he bears a close resemblance to the character commemorated by Edward Lear:

> There was a Young Person of Kew,
> Whose virtues and vices were few.[1]

---

[1] It is suggested to me that another Epicurean in the same collection of specimens is the Old Man of Hong-Kong, who never did anything wrong; he lay on his back, with his head in a sack, that innocuous Old Man of Hong-Kong. But the Old Man of Hong-Kong went too far. He forgot, for instance, Epicurus' precept: "We must laugh and philosophize at the same time and do our household duties and employ our other faculties" (B. Epic. fr. 41).

If the highest Pleasure is a static equilibrium, there is never any reason to enlarge our experience, whether physical, emotional, or mental. I will not begin to smoke, because I have got on so far quite well without it. I will not fall in love, because loving and losing would be more upsetting to emotional equilibrium than never having loved at all. I will not continue to study astronomy, because I am already convinced that the stars obey natural, not divine, laws, and there is therefore nothing further to be gained. Viewed in this light, the Epicurean state of equilibrium may well be considered the *safest* form of Pleasure, because the least at the mercy of outside circumstances and other people; but "nature barks out" that it is not the *highest* form of Pleasure. In direct contradiction of Epicurus we might say that the highest form of Pleasure is not something static but something that involves movement and expansion: the individual man finds his highest Pleasure in expanding the limits of his experience wider and wider, in increasing his range of sensibility; just as the species Man, with all his complexity of mind and body, has developed from the comparatively simple protoplasm.—Whether we define Pleasure in this or in some other way, enough has been said to show that here too Epicurus' definition falls far short. He failed to allow for man's inexhaustible spirit of adventure, and it is in the exercise of this spirit, whether in the sphere of bodily, emotional, or mental activity, that most men find, not their most secure, but their highest Pleasure.

NOTES ON PASSAGES 1–21

50. Lucr. is addressing Memmius. **quod superest:** a common formula in Lucr. to mark transition from one topic to another. Its force here is lost, since there is a lacuna immediately preceding.

51. **semotum a curis,** ἀταραξία being the Epicurean ideal.

55. **primordia rerum:** enter the hero, one might almost say, since the whole Epicurean Natura Rerum is based on the atom. *Primordia* and *principia* translate the Epicurean term ἀρχαί, "first-beginnings".

56 f. **unde** as often = *e quibus.* **quove** (for *quo-que*) = *et in quae*: a usage perhaps originating from a desire not to confuse the relative with *quisque.* **perempta,** sc. *primordia,* "at their perishing".

58 ff. Lucr. proceeds to give a list of his synonyms for *primordia.* **semina rerum** is a metaphor which by its ambiguity might have led to erroneous deductions: things come into being not by the unfolding of vital force within the "seeds" but merely through the aggregation of a number of "seeds".

60. **usurpare,** "name".

65. **super,** adv.

66. **Graius homo,** Epicurus.

70. **irritat,** rare contraction from *irritavit*: cf. VI. 587 *disturbat.*

72. **vivida vis...pervicit:** alliteration and assonance common in Lucr. and early Latin; cf. with this ex. Ennius, *Priamo vi vitam evitari.* They are used both for emphasis and as a natural ornament of language. Cf. Intro. p. xxvii.

73 f. **flammantia moenia mundi:** in both a literal and a metaphorical sense, because Epic. believed the "world" (*mundus,* including sun, moon and stars) to be spherical and surrounded by an outer belt of fiery ether. See v. 457–470.

processit, peragravit, subj. Epicurus.

omne, "the universe", in which are innumerable "worlds".

75 ff. **quid possit...haerens**: a vital passage which is repeated elsewhere in the *de R.N.* "If there is anything for which the world is indebted to Epic. (probably still more to Lucr.), it is for a clear enunciation of the principle of law in Nature" (Masson).

alte terminus haerens, "deep-set boundary stone", is a worthy metaphor to signify the limit set to everything by natural law. Man need suffer no more under fear of the unknown.

78. **vicissim,** "in *her* turn".

82. **indugredi,** archaic, like *indupedire, induperator*.

quod contra: whether *quod* is acc. after *contra* or the old form of the abl., *contra* being adv., is doubtful. In either case the meaning is, "whereas on the contrary".

86. **prima virorum**: a Greek touch, τὰ πρῶτα with a masc. gen. being common in Greek, the corresponding constr. rare in Latin.

87. **infula**: the band worn by the victim.

88. "and streamed in even lengths (*pari parte = pariter*) down either cheek".

92. **genibus summissa,** lit. "let down by her knees". "Sank to the earth on her knees."

93. **quibat,** subj. *quod*, etc.

94. Being his eldest child.

95 f. Iphigeneia had been summoned to Aulis on the pretext that she was to be married to Achilles. The terms used here by Lucr. contain a corresponding ambiguity, being applicable to the ceremonies both of marriage and of sacrifice, viz. *sublata virum manibus* (the ceremony of seizing the bride from her mother performed by the bridegroom's friends), *tremibunda* (of the bride or of the victim), *deductast* (the ceremony of escorting her to the bridegroom).

97. **comitari,** pass. **Hymenaeo**: for an ex. see Catullus, 61.

98. **casta** suggests the bride: **inceste** (with *concideret*) denotes the pollution of blood.

99. **parentis**: the father who should have given the bride away.

101. This great line can be set beside *Nil igitur mors est ad nos neque pertinet hilum* and *Mortalem vitam mors cum immortalis ademit* (III. 830, 869): it is one of the peaks of the *de R.N.*

102. tutemet: the double suffix is unusual.

iam quovis, lit. "presently at some time or another".

107. et merito, "not without cause" (do they conjure up dreams).

113. "whether the soul is born or on the other hand is implanted in us at birth". Body and soul acc. to Epic. are both corporeal: the soul is born and dies as a part of the body. Pythagoras and Platonists held that it came from without and entered the body at birth.

114. et simul intereat, "and also whether it...".

117. Ennius, who created Latin poetry as we know it by writing his *Annales* in the quantitative hexameter form imported from Greece, in place of the Saturnian rhythm used by Livius Andronicus in his transl. of the *Odyssey* and by Naevius in his *Bellum Punicum*.

Ennius held the Pythagorean doctrine of the transmigration of souls.

119. clueret: *clueo*, an archaic vb. frequently used by Lucr., sometimes = *audio* ("am named", Gk. ἀκούω), sometimes merely = *sum*. See Intro. p. xxv.

120. Although inconsistently with this (*praeterea tamen*) he maintains, etc.

127 ff. sum up the two main problems to be dealt with, which Lucr. has just been discussing: (*a*) the nature of celestial and terrestrial phenomena (which will be shown to have no connection with the *gods*), and (*b*) the nature of the soul (which is mortal, and *death* therefore holds no terrors for us). Connected with (*b*) is the problem of the appearance of the dead in disease and sleep: this too Lucr. will explain.

cum (l. 127) is picked up by *tunc* (l. 130): "both... and...".

bene...habenda...ratio, "we must reason well".

132 ff. It is noticeable here and elsewhere that one of the main indications of the survival of the soul after death that Lucr. felt called upon to refute, was the occurrence of *dreams* (or disordered visions) of the dead. There is little doubt that Lucr. was not endowed by nature with a mind at rest, that he was far from possessing the easy temperament of his master Epicurus.

This paragraph (ll. 127–135) well illustrates the Epicurean view of scientific enquiry. The motive is not the desire for knowledge for its own sake: scientific enquiry is only a means by which men may rid themselves of *fear*, and so win their way to ἀταραξία.

On both these points cf. IV. 26–45 (Passage 11).

2. I. 921–950

922. nec me animi fallit: a phrase occurring also at I. 136 and V. 97. Lit. "nor does it deceive me in mind". Cicero has *pendere animi*.

obscura, sc. *ea*, from *quod superest*.

acri...thyrso, "with sharp goad". *Thyrsus*, lit. "stem", is more often used of the Bacchic wand: and the use of the word here carries with it a suggestion of "frenzy", un-Epicurean though such frenzy be.

926–950 are repeated, with the exception of the last four words, as prooemium to Book IV.

avia Pieridum etc. This is to be understood in the limited sense indicated by V. 335–337, where Lucr. writes: "Again, this nature of things, this philosophy, is but lately discovered, and I myself was found the very first of all who could turn it into the speech of my country." The *de R.N.* was not the first philosophical poem in Latin, for Cicero had already translated the works of Aratus into hexameters: but Lucr. could justifiably claim that he was the first to turn the Epicurean philosophy into Latin poetry.

932. religionum...nodis: *religio* may be etymologically connected with *ligare*, "bind", as this passage suggests, or it may be similar to *negligo* (*nec-lego*, "not care for"). Lucr. naturally felt the force of the former connection.

935. ab, expressing origin. "Is seen to be not without good reason."

936. medentes, "healers".

937. circum with *pocula*.

939 ff. "that the unthinking age of children may be fooled as far as the lips, and meanwhile drink up the bitter draught of wormwood and though beguiled yet not be betrayed" (M.).

942. pacto=*modo* (cf. *nullo pacto*).

943. ratio, "philosophy".

944. quibus=*iis a quibus*.

950. compta, from *como* (=*co-emo*), "bring together".

figura, lit. "shape": its very general meaning here is perhaps best rendered by "pattern".

3. IV. 379–521

379. hic, "in this". Lucr. has been describing the way in which our shadow appears to accompany us about as though it were a real object, when in reality a moving shadow is merely air deprived of light through a series of successive points.

381. "whether the lights are the same lights" (as before).

383. Lucr.'s explanation is summarized in the n. on l. 379.

384. demum emphasizes *animi*. It is the duty of the *mind*, not of the senses.

387 f. Lucr. thinks of ships where we should naturally think of trains.

390. praeter with quos.

393. longos = *longinquos*.

397. extantes... montes is put first for emphasis, instead of *inter quos extantis montis*. The resulting anacoluthon presents little difficulty.

406. supra with quos and montis.

408 f. "are distant from us scarcely two thousand arrow flights, nay often scarcely...".

414. at here as often introduces an additional not a contrasting point.

digitum non altior unum: a construction usually restricted to *plus, minus, amplius, maior, minor*. See Madv. *LG.* 306. "Not deeper than a finger-breadth."

416. impete here denotes not force but extent.

419. corpora, if the text be right, = birds. Cf. Ennius, I. 33 (ed. Steuart): *cedunt de caelo ter quattuor corpora sancta | avium.*

420. denique, in Lucr. usually synonymous with *praeterea, porro* = "again", introducing a fresh argument.

421. despeximus in: a more usual constr. than the simple acc. in l. 418.

422 f. "a force seems to be carrying the body of the horse standing thus motionless athwart the stream and to be thrusting it swiftly up-current". *in adversum flumen* is explanatory of *transversum*.

424. omnia: all solid objects seen on either side of the stream (*traiecimus*). The stream itself appears for the moment to be stationary.

426 f. The sense is that from end to end of the portico

(*a*) the two sides are parallel, (*b*) roof and floor, being separated by pillars of equal length, are also parallel.

ductu, "line". Cf. Cic. *de rep.* II. 11: *tractus ductusque muri.* Cf. too *aquaeductus.*

427. stansque, *et est stans = et stat.*

428. "when it is viewed in its entire length from the upper end".

429. trahit, subj. *porticus.* An alternative to the more straightforward *trahitur in fastigia.*

fastigia, "sloping sides".

431. "until it has brought all together into the vanishing apex of the cone". The obj. of *conduxit* is understood from the preceding line.

Lucr. wrestles with *patrii sermonis egestas* in this description of perspective.

432 f. *fit nautis ut sol videatur.*

435. A reminder of the purpose of all these examples. The eyes cannot see beyond the horizon: it is the mind that is at fault if we believe that the sun sets in the sea.

436. clauda, "maimed". Or the opposite of *recta*, cf. l. 514.

437. aplustris: *aplustre* (plur. *aplustra* or *-ia*) = ἄφλαστον, the curved stern of a ship.

440. liquorem with obeunt.

441. sursumque supina reverti, "to be bent back upwards".

Emphatic reiteration of this kind is common in Lucr., cf. his description of a crooked house ll. 516 ff.

443 ff. Lucr. sets down his exx. in random order. This ex. is closely connected with that of the moving ship (l. 387) and the stationary horse (l. 420).

447. You have to press hard!

451. geminare intr. here. It is normally tr.

460. "austere silence": cf. v. 1190: *noctis signa severa.*

464. pars...maxima: it is strange that Lucr. is here less emphatic than Epic., who says that *all* such instances of illusion are due to the mind's additions (*Ep.* I. 50). Perhaps Lucr. implies that we are not always taken in.

466. "are accepted as seen".

469. siquis: Lucr. is thinking of the Sceptics and the New Academy.

470. scire, sc. *se.*

471. mittam = *omittam*. contendere causam, not a normal usage with *contendere*, but cf. *pugnare pugnam*.

472. Perhaps proverbial. Cf. Ter. *Ad.* 316: *capite in terram statuerem*, "I would plant him head downward on the ground". The Sceptic, acc. to Lucr., has no basis for his argument: he can't tell his head from his heels.

473. uti concedam, "to grant" (for the moment). scire, sc. *eum*.

475. undĕ sciat: the Augustan and post-Augustan poets (apart from the satirists) avoided having a short open vowel before a word beginning with *sc-*, *sp-*, etc.

476. notitiam: the concept (πρόληψις) is the result of a number of sense-perceptions or experiences. If a man has had no experience of "knowing" or of "the true", how can he have the concept of knowledge or of truth?

478. primis, emphatic: *ab sensibus ut primis*.

478 f. The fundamental axiom of Epicureanism.

480 ff. The general meaning is: if the senses are to be refuted, something of greater authority must be found, something that can establish the truth independently of outside assistance. But Reason will not qualify for this task. Nor can one sense be used to refute another.

483. falso, as Lucr.'s imagined opponent maintains.

485. Bailey quotes Democritus: "Wretched mind," say the senses, "from us you received your belief, yet you overthrow us; your victory is your defeat."

493. Cf. II. 742, 743: *corpora...nullo coniuncta colore*, where Lucr. is drawing a distinction between form and colour. quaecumque etc. refers then to all the varieties of form which we see in addition to varieties of colour. videre merely repeats *sentire*.

498. aequa fides: given identical conditions. For if we move nearer, the passage between the mountains (ll. 397–399) becomes visible and the eyes refute the eyes.

500. dissolvere, "explain", "unravel".

501. Refers to an optical illusion mentioned at l. 353: square towers look round from a distance.

502. praestat, "it is better".

503. mendose: that is, be content to offer an explanation not necessarily true. The Epicurean accepts any explanation as hypothetically true, provided it is not contradicted by the evidence of the senses. See pp. 15 ff.

504. "than to let slip away from your hands things manifest". **quoquam**, lit. "anywhither".

508. **ausis** = *velis*, as often in Plaut.

508 ff. Characteristic of Epic.'s appeal to the common sense of the plain man.

513 ff. The simile is natural to an Epicurean: Epic. called his fundamental axioms "Canonic", from κανων = *regula*. This perhaps partly accounts for the emphatic reiteration in these lines, esp. l. 517.

515. **libella**: a π-shaped or triangular instrument, from the top of which hung a plumb-line.

519. **iudiciis**, "measurements".

520. **ratio...rerum**, "reasoning of things".

521. **falsis**: see n. on l. 483.

*4. VI. 703–737

704. **sit**, sc. *causa*, the cause.

707. **illius una** = *illius hominis leti una causa*, "the one cause of...".

708. **vincere**, "prove".

711. **habemus**, "can", Gk. ἔχομεν.

712. "towards summer"; implying also "every summer" (*in diem*).

713. Bailey places a comma after *terris* and translates, "the N., the river of all Egypt, alone in the world rises, as summer comes,...". But *Aegypti totius amnis* seems feeble. The force of *unicus in terris Aegypti totius amnis* will be appreciated by anyone who happens to have seen aerial photographs of the Nile valley.

716. **quī** shortened and unelided before a vowel: with monosyllables not uncommon in Lucr., and occurs in Virgil. See M. II. 404 n.

etesiač, less common: see l. 743.

The etesians were trade winds blowing every year (ἔτος) during the summer.

718. **replent**: *fluvium* is the obj.

725. **oppilare**, tr., as in the other two passages where it occurs in Latin. **ostia** with oppilare. **contra**, adv. **fluctibus adversis** here either of the river or of the sea. "...drifts

of sand may block up the outflow as a bar against the
opposing waves, when the sea...rolls the sand in."

726. **ruit**, tr. Cf. Hor. *Sat.* II. v. 22. Lit. "rake together".

5. I. 418–482

418. Lit. to begin again to weave my design in words;
"to weave again at the web, which is the task of my discourse" (B.).

419. The prose order would be *omnis igitur natura, ut
est per se.*

422. **per se esse**, "exists". **communis sensus**, "feeling
common to all men".

423. **cui** dependent on *fides*.

425. All reasoning is ultimately based on the senses.

429. Footnotes had not been invented: hence this most
prosaic of all Lucr.'s hexameters.

432. **numero**, redundant.

433. "whatever shall *exist*, must be something in itself".
In saying this Lucr. really assumes what is to be proved.

434. "if it admit of touch".

435. **dum sit**, "if it exist at all": an unnecessary repetition. "It will increase the amount of matter by an addition
either..., and will go with the sum total."

440 f. Will either act or be acted upon, and in either case
will be matter.

447. **sub sensus cadat**, "fall within the ken of our senses".

449 f. **his rebus**, matter and void.

452. **discidio**: without the destruction of that to which
the "property" belongs.

453. **liquor**, "liquidity", "wetness", not "liquid".
Notice *liquor*: *liquor* is the usual quantity.

459. The nature of Time provides a special problem,
which is discussed in the running commentary.

460. **consequitur** may here be tr. (with *quid* clause) or
intr. (*quid* clause dependent on *sensus*).

462. **per se** with **tempus**.

463. **motu placidaque quiete**: the state of motion and
the state of rest.

464 ff. The problem of the nature of past events.

Lucr. first warns us against a quibble which may be introduced owing to the structure of the infin. pass. in Latin.
Tyndaridem raptam ESSE dicunt = (*a*) "they say Helen was
carried off", (*b*) "they say the carrying off of Helen is",
i.e. exists as an entity. Transl. "is a fact", in order to bring
out the ambiguity.

467. **quando,** causal. "...to admit that these things
exist in themselves because...."

469. **terris...regionibus,** difficult: one naturally asks,
what is the difference? B. translates, "an accident in one
case of the countries, in another even of the regions of
space". This is the best that can be done without emendation of the text.

Lucr. gives a double answer to the imagined objectors.
(1) Past events are "accidents" of the locality where they
occurred (ll. 469, 470). (2) They must also be "accidents"
of those material objects (e.g. Paris, the wooden horse)
which played a necessary part in bringing them about
(ll. 471–482). But he does not explain *our present consciousness* of such events, which is the crux of the problem. For
this see running commentary.

476. **Troianis** either abl. with **clam,** or dat. (*clam,* adv.).
A native reader or writer would hardly bother to distinguish.
durateus = δουράτεος.

480. A circumlocution for "nor are they the same as
void".

481. **sed magis,** sc. *ita esse.*

6. I. 951–983

952. **volitare:** he does not in fact teach us about the
constant motion of the atoms till Book II.

953. **finis,** "limit".

958. **omne quod est** = τὸ πᾶν, the universe. Take which-
ever of the roads through the universe you please, at no
point in any of them will you reach its bound (M.). "The
roads through the universe never come to an end; for then
the universe would of necessity have an extreme point."

961 f. **videatur,** sc. *illud* or *finis;* "so that a bound is
seen further than which this sense of ours cannot follow
the thing": viz. a point at which *A* ends and *B* begins.

966. **usque adeo,** "so true it is that".

967. **infinitum,** pred. **omne,** "the whole".

970. **ultimus** merely emphasizes *ad extremas oras*.

977. **probeat** for *prohibeat*.

978. **finique locet se,** (causes it to fail to) "find its mark". Such ablatives in *-i* are common in Lucr.

979. **foras,** outward and onward. **fine,** the limit of the universe.

981. **fiat** followed by *fiet uti* in a different sense.

983. **fugae copia** together: "room for flight ever extends the chance of flight".

7. II. 216–293

217. **corpora** = *corpora prima*. **rectum,** used adverbially.

218. **ferme,** "at quite uncertain times".

219. **depellere,** intr.: "they drive aside a little from their course". For a similar use of *spatium*, cf. IV. 1196.

225. There follows a piece of sound and perspicacious reasoning.

232. **corpus aquae naturaque...aeris** = *aqua et aer*.

239. **aeque concita,** "at equal speed though with unequal weights".

243. **etiam atque etiam,** "again and again I say".

248. **quod** = *quoad* or *quantum*.

250. If the text be right we can but take *sese* with *declinare* and consider the curious order·to be an ex. of Lucr.'s negligence or of the unrevised state in which he left his work. *declinare* again takes an acc. at l. 259. "But that nothing at all can swerve from the straight line of its path, who is there who can descry?"

254. **fati foedera:** Lucr. attacks what we now call Determinism.

260. **ubi,** "when and where". **tulit mens:** cf. III. 44: *si fert ita forte voluntas.*

261 f. "gives each man a beginning of these movements" (lit. "for these things").

263. **tempore puncto:** a common phrase in Lucr. = *temporis puncto*: while the smallest point of time is pricked down or marked (M.).

264. **carceribus:** the barrier at the starting-place of a racecourse.

267. concīta, though *concīta* at l. 239.

269. initum: *initus* for *initium*.

corde, because it was the seat of the *animus*. The process mentioned here is more fully described in the following book.

270. id is strange: *movere*, the general idea of movement, must be understood from *motus*.

288 f. Weight is the primary cause of the motion of the atoms. But the downward motion which it produces precludes the possibility of their striking against one another unless we assume an "internal" force in each atom causing it to swerve. Once that is assumed, then *plagae* come in as a third cause of atomic motion.

289 f. necessum intestinum, "an inner necessity". It is unusual to find *necessum* with an epithet: unusual too to find it with *habere*.

292. id, sc. *ne...habeat*.

*8. II. 333–407

335. multigenis: here only, but Lucr. also has *alienigena*, *terrigena*, etc.

336. non quo (*non quod, non quin* are used similarly) parum multa: "not that a scanty number...but that (or because)...." It is usual to have as here the subj. in the first clause, the indic. in the second.

There is, as he afterwards shows, an infinite number of atoms of each shape, although the number of different shapes is limited and there is both a minimum and a maximum limit to their size.

337. vulgo with omnia: "they are not all without exception the same one with another".

341. filo: *filum*, lit. "texture", comes also to mean "thickness" and here prob. = "size", though it may perhaps only be synonymous with *figura*.

342 ff. What he now proceeds to say provides both analogy and proof. The uniqueness of every single creature or object that we know in this world illustrates by analogy the differences in the shapes of the atoms: it also proves that these differences must exist, for how else could any object composed of atoms be uniquely distinct from its fellows?

genus humanum, etc: *nominativi pendentes*, but the sense
is clear.

344. laetantia, prob. "gladdening".

347. "of these go and take any one you will from amongst
its kind". generatim is hardly adequate to bring out the
point, namely that individuals differ within the kind, as
well as kind from kind.

351. nota: neut. as referring to animals in general.
cluere, "are clearly".

352 ff. Lucr. is perhaps killing two birds with one stone
by using an ex. which suggests the cruelty of religion.

356. *quaerit* is perhaps the most likely emendation suggested for *non quit*.

359. adsistens, "stopping". crebra: used adverbially.

363. subitam describes the recurrent pang. Throughout
this passage Lucr. implies the homogeneity of human and
animal feelings: the universe is all of one stuff, as we saw
with special clearness in the doctrine of the atomic swerve.

370. fere, "commonly", "always".

371. tamen responds to *quodvis*: take any kind you like,
yet....

372. quique, abl.: attracted to *suo genere*. "You will not
find that every grain, each in its several kind, is like the rest."

376. pavit (*pavire*), "beats": cf. Gk. παίειν.

380. quaedam, sc. *primordia*. Some are different, others
like.

381. animi ratione: we pass from the analogy provided
by things known to us through our senses, to its application
by the *mind* to things beyond the range of the senses, i.e.
the atoms.

383. fuat: archaic form = *sit*.

387. hĭc (nom. pron.): short as in several other places
in Lucr., rarely later. It is, however, normal in early Latin.

388. cornum, "horn-lantern". Unusual form of *cornu*.

391. colum, "strainer".

395 f. *tam repente inter se* (i.e. *from* each other) *diducta*.

401. centauri, gen. of *centaurium* (usu. *centaureum*) =
"centaury", a plant. pertorquent, "twist awry".

404. quaĕ amara: cf. VI. 716 n. (Passage 4).

406. "tear open passages into our senses" (dat.).

407. corpus: i.e. that part of the body's surface through
which they enter.

9. III. 94–160

94. animum. *animus, mens, consilium* are used as synonyms by Lucr. His discussion of *anima* begins at l. 117.

97–98. Between these lines a line is lost, the sense of which must have been "But some philosophers have supposed...".

99. habitum (ἕξις), "state", "condition". The nature of *habitus vitalis* is explained in the following lines.

100. harmoniam Grai. Lucr. is referring particularly to Aristoxenus, a pupil of Aristotle and a writer on the theory of music. Music is produced by the attunement of the strings of the instrument: Aristoxenus used this example as an illustration of the relationship between mind and body. In the *Phaedo* Simmias maintains that the soul is ἁρμονία τις.

105. diversi, "astray".

115. multimodis. Cic. *Orator*, 153: *saepe brevitatis causa contrahebant ut ita dicerent, "multi' modis"*. Lucr. often uses *omnimodis = omnibus modis*.

118. harmonia, by means of a harmony.

121. corpora = *corpora prima*, atoms.

122. aer and (ll. 126, 128) *ventus* are used loosely here, though carefully distinguished ll. 231 ff.

124–125. "have an equal part to play".

132–134. The name Harmony, either a gift to musicians from the Muses, or perhaps wrested by them from something else and transferred in *illam rem quae tum nomine proprio egebat*. Heliconi, abl. M. collects similar exx. from Lucr. in his note on l. 978.

135. habeant contemptuously: "let them keep it". *Sibi habeant* is common in this sense.

136. coniuncta, neut., referring to two nouns of different genders: a common though not obligatory usage.

138. quasi with caput.

143. animae used here loosely as including, being of the same essential stuff as, *animus*. *Anima* has to do duty both for τὸ ἄλογον and for ἡ ψυχή.

144. paret, sc. *animo* or *menti*.

154 ff. sudoresque etc. A passage reminiscent of Sappho's famous ode and the translation or adaptation of it by Catullus (51).

*10. III. 231–322

231. natura, sc. *animi animaeque*.

234. calor and *vapor* are used as synonyms by Lucr.

239. "since the mind does not admit that any of these can...".

240. The text is uncertain, but the meaning of the line was doubtless "the motions that cause sensation and the mind's (own) thoughts".

247. venti synonymous with *aura* (l. 232).

caeca, "invisible". The other three components are of course equally invisible.

251. contrarius ardor: *ardor* may refer to any strong emotion, pleasant or unpleasant. *Contrarius* makes the meaning clear.

252. temere, "lightly", i.e. without doing serious injury.

huc...usque: either (1) referring back to the *quarta natura* of ll. 241–246. No *injury* can be done to the *quarta natura* without proving fatal. The objection to this way of taking it is that Lucr. has already told us that the *quarta natura* receives every sensation *first*. But he may be referring here exclusively to the *quarta natura* of the centrally situated *animus*, and thinking of a shock so violent as to injure it irreparably. Or (2), referring to l. 250, =*in ossa atque medullas*.

254. "life is ousted".

256. quasi, here and at II. 958, perhaps =*paene*.

257. motibus: the *motus* referred to at ll. 245, 247.

258. No caesura. M. suggests: "The verse may have prompted a Latin to pronounce *interse se*."

259. aventem, sc. *me*.

262. principiorum, used by Lucr. as the gen. of *primordia*, is to be taken here with *motibus*, i.e. *motibus suis*.

265. vis, plur.

266. quod genus, an archaic phrase =*velut*.

268. unum corporis augmen, "the bulk of a single body".

271. "gives out to them from itself".

274. infra, not literally distant from the surface of the body, but secret, eluding analysis. Cf. IV. 111, 112: *primordia tantum | sunt infra nostros sensus....*

276 ff. The *quarta natura* is to the other three components of the *animus* and *anima*, as the *animus* and *anima* are to the rest of the body.

280. quasi: Lucr., speaking more exactly, moderates the metaphor he used at l. 275. Epic. issued a warning against the use of metaphor (Epic. *Ep.* I. 38).

284. Now one, now another of the three components is more hidden or more prominent, as Lucr. explains at ll. 288 ff.

285. ut=*ita tamen ut.* Yet so that all the components make up one single substance.

286. ni=*ne* (cf. *nive*, II. 734).

287. Sensation is only possible when all the components are present.

288. etiam: *animus* as well as *anima* possesses *calor.*

299. magis with ventosa.

302. "draws its life from...".

303. percit for *perciet*: cf. VI. 410, *concit.*

306. interutrasque: *utrasque,* adv. on the analogy of *alias, alteras. interutrasque* is used only by Lucr., but used by him seven times (cf. II. 518, V. 472, 476, 839, VI. 362, 1062).

cervos, leones in apposition as though he had written *inter utrosque.*

308. illa, neut. plur.

315. sequaces, either "clinging" or "that follow on from their natures".

317. quot, sc. *figurae.*

II. IV. 26–109

26–32 summarize the content of Books I–III.

32. quove=*quo-que*: see I. 56 n. (Passage 1).

ordia prima=*primordia*: only here.

34. simulacra=εἴ)ωλα. *imagines* and *effigiae* are both synonyms of *simulacra,* Lucr.'s use of the terms varying according to metrical requirements.

35. "like films peeled off from the surface of things" (M.).

37–45 explain the *vementer* of l. 33. The theory of Idols has a vital bearing on the question of the nature of the Soul, because by this theory we can explain the mental visions that are sometimes formed, whether in waking life or in sleep, of the dead. The importance which Lucr. attached

to the problem of dreams of the dead has already been noted
(I. 132 n.). Here he makes this problem the *raison d'être*
of Book IV.

41. ne...reamur: dependent on *nunc agere incipiam*.

45. discessum dederint = *discesserint*.

50. cortex, "rind".

51. eius, after *similem*. "...like to that, whatever it be,
from whose body it is shed and wanders forth" (M.).

52. cluet: I. 119 n. (Passage I).

55. diffusa solute, i.e. without preserving the shape of
the thing.

56. vaporem, "heat".

59. membranas, "cauls". The caul is a membranous
covering: it is sometimes found remaining round the head
of a human child after birth.

63. debet is hardly justifiable: the "proof" has been
based merely on a loose analogy.

65. illa, sc. *tunicae*, etc.

66. hiscendist nulla potestas, "we cannot utter a word
to show why...". *hiscere*, lit. "open the mouth".

70, 71 contain two reasons why the Idols can be cast off
"the more quickly": (1) because they are inconceivably
thin and therefore are composed of but few atoms, (2) because these atoms are already on the outermost surface of
the object and are therefore not hemmed in or knocked
back by their fellow-atoms.

72. iacere ac largiri: the obj. of these verbs is sup-
pressed, viz. *corpora* or *primordia*.

73. ut diximus ante: see the exx. given at l. 56.

74. de summis = *de summis rebus*, or (since *multa* is
subj. of the sentence and = *multae res*) *de se summis*.

76. ferrugina: "steel-blue" is probably our equivalent.
Greeks and Romans saw colour through eyes different from
ours and it is notoriously difficult to translate some of their
colour-words, πορφύρεος, *caeruleus*, etc. In English we have
a larger number of colour-words than in Greek or Latin:
but even so the tongue still lags far behind the eye and we
can still give only a blurred colour-picture through the
medium of words.

77. vulgata, "spread out" before the people's gaze.

78. consessum caveai, "the assembly on the benches".
subter, adv.

79. **scaenai speciem,** "the bravery of the stage" (B.).

coetumque: *-quę* misplaced. The senators occupied the seats in the orchestra.

80. The colours shed by the awnings on the people below shift as the awnings are stirred by the wind.

82. **moenia,** "hoardings": Roman theatres were still built of wood in Lucr.'s day. **haec...omnia** ref. to *consessum*, etc.

86. "since in either case (i.e. both *lintea* and *res quaeque*) they are discharging from the surface".

87. **vestigia,** "traces".

88. **filo,** lit. = "thickness". "Of an exquisite fineness."

89. The Idols cast off by any given object follow one another with extreme rapidity. The eye, receiving this rapid succession of Idols, cannot see any one of them separately but only the series. Similarly, when we watch a film at the cinema we do not see any one of the individual photographs separately, but only the moving picture formed by the series of individual photographs. Cf. IV. 768–776.

91. **diffusae:** emphatic, in contrast to *vestigia certa* (l. 87).

93. "They are torn on their tortuous course." The atoms of smell, etc., arising from deep within an object, are on their way out diverted again and again from their course by the blows of their fellow atoms: thus they issue forth as a *shapeless* collection of atoms.

recta, "straight".

94. **coortae,** "in one mass".

98. **speculis,** sc. *in.* "In mirrors, in water, and in every bright surface."

101. **ea,** acc. neut. plur. "That they are formed of the emitted images of things."

106. **cum...tamen,** "although...yet". **repulsu:** from the surface of the mirror.

108. **nec ratione alia** etc.: that is, if there were no *tenues effigiae,* or if the *effigiae* were not *assiduo crebroque repulsu reiectae* from the reflecting surface, the formation of reflections exactly corresponding to the object reflected would be impossible.

videntur, sc. *effigiae.*

109. **tanto opere** with **similes.**

*12. V. 564–591

564. nimio here means no more than *multo*.

nec minor ardor: but no one is likely to suppose that
the sun is *less* bright than it appears to be. Similarly
minores at l. 590 seems to be unnecessary. See n. on l. 573.

566. quibus...cumque, together. ignes, nom.

567. adicere: "cast to us their light".

568. illa, sc. *spatia*. his intervallis, "because of the
intervening space": tautological.

569. nil, adverbial acc. Also at l. 588 (*perparvum quiddam*).

571. loca: those parts of the body affected by heat and light.

572. hinc, "from the earth". filum, "size". videri...
vere, "be seen as it really is".

573. nil adeo=*nil admodum*, "practically nothing".
"You could alter it almost nothing to greater or less" (B.):
alternatively *plus aut minus* may be our colloquial "more or
less", as in the quotation from Enn. on p. xxviii. Similarly
Gk. οὐδὲ μείζων οὐδὲ ἐλάττων.

575. notho, "bastard", "not its own".

577. "however that may be".

578. In full: *quam ea figura* (nom.), *qua lunam ferri
cernimus, esse videtur.*

580. specie confusa, "blurred in appearance". The
meaning of *species* here is distinct from its meaning at l. 569.

581 ff. *necesse est luna nobis hinc* (=*e terra*) *videatur
utcumque* (=*talis qualiscumque*) *est, oris extremis notata*
("clear-cut in outline"), *quantaque quantast* (=*et quanta-
cumque est*). With *quantus quantus* cf. *quisquis*=*quicumque.*

585. quoscumque etc. with scire licet (l. 590), ll. 586–
589 being parenthetical.

589. "to less or greater, the further they are away".
Strict logic would require "or the nearer they are" to be
added.

13. V. 925–1240

929. *quod* (=*quippe quod*, as at l. 926) *non facile ex aestu*
etc. *caperetur.* "Could not easily be affected by...."

930. labi: archaic form of the abl.

934. scibat: archaic form (*metri gratia*) for *sciebat.*
molirier arva, "work the fields".

943. "the flowering youth of the world" (B.).

945. vocabant with the infin.: a rare use.

947. clarus, lit. "clearly-heard". "The loud waterfall."
948. vagi, nom. plur. templa, "haunts".
949 f. *e quibus* (sc. *templis*) *fluenta...lavere sciebant.*
951. stillantia with saxa. super = "down over": the abl. here is a poetical use.
953. Lit. "manage things with the help of fire". "Turn fire to use."
961. "live and thrive for himself alone".
970. sŭbus, but *sŭbus* at VI. 974, 977. Dat. plur. of *sus.*
971 f. "overtaken by night". circum, adv.
975 f. "bided the time when the sun should...".
977. "from childhood": a phrase also used by Cicero.
979 f. mirarier, diffidere: both used as subjects to *posset.*
983. "made sleep dangerous".
988. nimio here = *multo.* "In much greater numbers."
989. lamentis, for *cum lamentis.*
990. enim: the reason for his statement in ll. 988, 989 does not in fact begin till l. 999, *at non....* "Then more often (magis) would a single one of them be seized and...."
993. A rhetorical conceit worthy of Ovid or Lucan: it is surprising in Lucr.
997. vermina: this rare word means "writhings" according to an ancient lexicographer, but "worms" suits the context better and may well be right.
998. vellent, "wanted", "needed"; or, "meant", "involved" (cf. Ovid, *Her.* XI. 96; more usu. *sibi velle,* L. and S. *s.v. volo* E 4 b δ).
1002. hic = *tum.* temere incassum frustra: one of Lucr.'s frequent emphatic pleonasms.
1005. in fraudem, "to his hurt".
1006. "the reckless art...lay undiscovered".
1007. tum deinde, emphatic *tum.*
1010. vergebant, lit. "turn", "incline" (tr.): hence "pour".
1011. ignem: this (according to Darwin the greatest discovery, except language, made by man) is more fully discussed, ll. 1091–1104.
1013. cognita sunt: at least one line, supplying the subject, must be lost. M. suggests, "*hospitium, ac lecti socialia iura duobus*".

1015. **curavit ut**=*effecit ut*. **alsia**, adj. from *algeo*, "cold".

1016. **non ita iam**, "no longer as before".

1022. **balbe**: the Social Contract is prior to the full use of language. Epic. avoids the unreality that appears in Hobbes' theory of the Social Contract, of supposing that the terms of the Social Contract were put into so many words by primitive man (Guyau).

1025. **bona magnaque**, just as we say "a good part".

1027. **propago**, "breeding".

1028, 1029. **natura**=φύσις. **utilitas**, implying both "use" and "advantage", refers to the later stage, when θέσις began to operate and men *agreed* to use certain sounds to indicate certain things.

1030, 1031. "speechlessness of tongue is seen to drive children on".

1033. **vis**: acc. plur. The acc. with *utor* and its compounds is an archaism. **abuti**, here "use", not "abuse". **quoad**, scanned as one syllable (by "synizesis"), = *quatenus*.

1035. **illis**: either *cornibus* (as though they were already there), or *frontibus*. **petit**, "butts".

1040. **auxiliatum** (only here) for *auxilium*.

1045. **tempore eodem** is merely equivalent to *tamen* (cf. v. 756, 765) and goes not with *facere* but with *putentur*.

1047. **notities** = πρόληψις (see under Canonic). A characteristic Epicurean argument, used also at l. 182 to disprove the creation of man by the gods. It is impossible to create a thing unless the creator already has a πρόληψις of it founded on previous sense-perceptions. Contrast Plato's theory of Ideas.

1049. **sciret**: an ex. of the lengthening of a syllable in arsis (a syllable on which the beat falls).

1054. **amplius**, "any more": implying once is enough. **auris**, acc. after *obtundere*.

1055. **inauditos**, "unheard before".

1063. **Molossum**, gen. plur.: they were large dogs from Epirus.

1064. **ricta**: *rictus* (or *rictum*), lit. = the open mouth. Here "lips".

1065. **rabie restricta**, "drawn back in rage".

1066. **et** for *atque* after *alio*.

1068. **morsuque** begins a new clause.

1069. **suspensis,** "kept in .check". **teneros imitantur haustus,** "*gently pretend to bite*".

1070. "fondle them with yelping sounds".

1071. **et,** as at l. 1066.

1074. **iuvencus,** here adj.

1076. **sub** is difficult, and other edd. read *ubi*.

1077. **sic,** "as may happen", "maybe". **alias,** adv.

1079. "hawks and ospreys and gulls".

1082. **praedaque:** *et de praeda.*

1083. **partim,** "some of them". **tempestatibus,** "the weather".

1088. **tamen** is out of place and logically goes with *emittere.*

1091. **illud,** "this", i.e. the question, Whence came fire? suggested by its mention at l. 1011.

1093. **primitus,** adv. "first".

1095. **fulgĕre** as though 3rd decl. Lucr. also has *fulgit,* "it lightens".

donavit vapore, "has endowed them with heat".

1096. **et tamen,** "yet also", apart from lightning. Cf. l. 1177.

1099. **emicat...:** connecting particle omitted.

1100. **mutua,** used here as adv.

1105. **hi,** the antecedent of *qui,* l. 1107.

1112. "and strength was held in honour".

1113. "property was invented and...".

1116. "however strong...". **creti,** perf. ptcp. of *cresco,* as though it were deponent.

1117 ff. show how far the word Epicurean has departed from its original meaning.

1119. "lack of a little".

1120. Cicero uses the same elliptical construction.

1124. **viai** adds nothing to *iter.*

1127. "the heights are set on fire": *vaporo* is usually transitive.

1128. **quae...cumque,** together.

1130. **regere imperio res:** recalled in Virgil's famous line *tu regere imperio populos, Romane, memento (Aen.* VI. 851).

1131. "let them sweat (with) blood".

1134. **ex auditis,** "from hearsay". **sensibus:** the supreme court of appeal.

1135. **id,** sc. ambition and its concomitants: it is of no greater worth now than it ever was. **magis est**: cf. Lucr.'s similar use of *clam est*.

1136. The history of Rome is doubtless in his mind.

1138. **insigne** used as noun, "emblem", i.e. the crown.

1140. **metutum**, perf. ptcp., only here.

1141. "And so things would pass to the utmost dregs of disorder" (B.). **summam faecem** shows that *faex* had become a dead metaphor. M. compares Petronius, *Sat.* 78, *ibat res ad summam nauseam*.

1142. **summatum**, "leadership": only here.

1143. **partim**: cf. l. 1083.

1144. **constituēre**, perf. ind.

1145. "tired of living by violence": *defessus* + infin. is a rare constr.

1148. **quod enim**, out of the natural order.

1151. **inde metus...**, i.e. fear of vengeance.

1151–1160. For discussion of the views expressed here see p. 96.

1154. **degere**, sc. *eum*. The Epicurean ideal.

1156. **divum**: Lucr. is using a popular phrase: the Epicurean gods had no concern with human affairs.

1157. **perpetuo** with **fore clam** (with which cf. l. 1135).

1158. **se** with protraxe (=*protraxisse*), "betrayed themselves".

1160. **in medium dedisse**, "made public".

1162. **ararum**, gen. after *compleverit*, as we say "full of...".

1164. **rebus**, here perhaps "occasions".

1167. **celebrare**, "throng".

1168. **non ita...**, "not very hard". **rationem reddere** *quae causa* etc.

1169. **iam tum**: in the early days of mankind.

1170. **animo vigilante**: in day-dreams, not with the eyes. See p. 54.

1171. **magis**, sc. *videbant*.

1174. **pro**, "befitting".

1175. **aeternamque** etc.: Lucr. implies that in contrast to mythological stories, in which gods bestow immortality on men, the truth is that men have bestowed immortality on the gods.

1176. Similar visions constantly re-appeared.

1177. **et tamen**: same use as at l. 1096. Apart from their constant re-appearance, their evident size and strength gave grounds for thinking them immortal. omnino emphasizes the importance of the reason given in the *quod* clause.

1182. ipsos, sc. *deos.* "And yet suffer no weariness." 1183 introduces the second cause of religion.

1187. tradere, facere, used as acc. subst. in apposition with *perfugium.*

1188. templa = *loca*, cf. l. 948.

1190. severa, "austere", denoting the purity and coldness of the starlight; Keats speaks of "the earnest stars" (Duff). Cf. IV. 460 (Passage 3): *severa silentia noctis.*

1203. Imitation of the gods' calmness of mind is the truest form of worship. See p. 87.

1205. super stellisque, *et super stellis.*

1206. venit in mentem: impers. + gen. (*viarum*), a constr. used by Cicero. Cf. *reminiscor* + gen.

1209. nobis, "over us".

1212. ecquaenam, dependent on *dubiam.*

1213. quoad, see n. to l. 1033.

1214. solliciti motus, together.

1216. "gliding down the never-ending track of years".

1223. corripiunt membra, "shrink into themselves".

1225. poenarum solvendi, a curious mixture of two constructions: *poenas solvendi* (gerund) and *poenarum solvendarum* (gerundive). M. cites a number of parallels, e.g. *facultas agrorum condonandi* (Cicero).

1228. pariter cum, together.

1229. quaesit, archaic pres. The 1st pers. *quaeso* survived longer.

1230. "a lull (*paces* plur. not uncommon) in the storm and favouring breezes".

1232. vada, an intentional ambiguity: both the literal and the metaphorical meaning is felt.

1233. vis abdita quaedam: speaking as a scientific philosopher Lucr. could hardly justify this phrase, but here he is writing with the emotion of a poet rather than with the reason of a philosopher.

1239. relinquunt, "leave in place", "admit".

14. V. 146–155

146. **illud**, sc. *sedis esse* etc.

147. **mundi**, "world", not "universe".

149. **animi mente**, emphatic for *mente* alone or *animo*. The Idols of the gods cannot be seen by the physical eye but only by the mind. See p. 54.

videtur, as often, pass.

150 f. "It follows that it (sc. *natura deum*) cannot touch anything (**nil contingere debet**) that can be touched by us (**tactile nobis**)." The gods, though not beyond the range of mental vision, are beyond the range of touch.

154. **de**, "after the manner of".

15. III. 14–24

14. **tua**: Lucr. is apostrophizing Epicurus. **ratio**, "philosophy".

16, 17. **moenia mundi discedunt**: the Epicurean is enabled to apprehend what is outside the compass of the world, e.g. the abodes of the gods.

inane, lit. "void", here the whole of Space, including atoms as well as void.

18 ff. A transl. of Homer's description of Olympus, *Od.* VI. 42 ff. Tennyson also takes it over in *Morte d'Arthur.*

divum numen, "the majesty of the gods".

16. II. 1090–1104

1090. **quae** refers to the truth that Lucr. has been demonstrating, that there are numberless other worlds in the universe besides ours.

1092. **dis expers**, "without the gods' aid".

1093. **pro** (or *proh*), exclamatory: "by the holy hearts of the gods,...who is able to...?"

1095. **immensi, profundi**, used as nouns.

1096. **indu**=*in*, cf. *induperator*. **moderanter habere**= *moderari.*

1097. caelos, plur., because it refers to the many skies of the many worlds: similarly terras.

1098. suffire, here only = "warm": elsewhere it = "perfume" or "fumigate". From *sufflo* ($fio = \theta\acute{v}\omega$).

1100. caeli serena, the expanse of sky above the clouds.

1104. inque merentis = *et immerentis.*

17. II. 1–33

1. mari magno, abl.

4. *sed quia cernere suave est ea mala quibus* etc.

7, 8. *templa serena, doctrinā sapientum edita et bene munita.*

16. "the little of life there is".

nonne videre: infin. expressing indignation, as often in Cicero. *Non* could replace *nonne* without affecting the sense.

17-19. The Epicurean definition of "passive pleasure" is here clearly enunciated.

17. sibi may refer to the subj. of *videre*, sc. *homines*, or to *naturam* (here = human nature). latrare, a vigorous metaphor: "cries out for". utqui = *ut. qui* here = $\pi\omega s$, cf. *atqui*, "but somehow", and in Plautus *hercle qui.*

18. absit, subj. *dolor*. fruatur, sc. *natura.*

21. quae etc.: explanatory of *pauca*. "Few things, namely such as...."

22. quoque: besides taking away pain they (sc. *pauca*) bring positive pleasure.

23 ff. Nature herself does not feel the want of any greater pleasure, although there are no golden images etc. (parenthesis from *si non* to *aurataque templa*), when (l. 29) men lie in groups, etc.

interdum looks forward to *cum*: "on the occasions when...." tamen (l. 29) is not needed, but it is suggested by the sense of the parenthesis.

24, 25. A form of lighting mentioned by Homer (*Od.* VII. 100 ff.).

27. fulgēt: the syllable is lengthened in arsis.

28. citharae: dat. with *reboant.*

31. corpora curant, "refresh themselves": used by Livy of a resting army.

18. VI. 58–79

58–66, repeated from v. 82–90. This may be a sign of lack of revision, but it is doubtful whether Lucr. would in any case have taken steps to avoid such repetition. It is inevitable that anyone who sets forth a system of philosophy should traverse some parts of the ground more than once.

64–66. See n. to I. 75 ff. (Passage 1).

69. putare: used as acc. subst. after *remittis*.

71. non quo, "not that...".

72. petere imbibat, "conceives the thought of exacting".

73. "You will imagine in your heart" (*tibi constitues*). quietos, sc. *deos*.

75 ff. describe the true nature of Epicurean worship.

76. simulacra, the Idols (see Passage 11).

78. suscipere, "drink in".

19. III. 830–977

830. igitur: without this word the line which is the climax of Book III would lose half its force. *igitur* adds to the mere statement the weight of the twenty-eight preceding proofs of the mortality of the soul.

831. habetur=*intellegitur* (M.); or perhaps "is but a mortal possession" (B.).

832. aegri, gen. after *nil*.

836, 837 contain a type of inversion common in Lucr. *omnes humani in dubio fuere utrorum ad regna cadendum sibi esset.*

839. uniter apti: a Lucretian expression, "made one".

843, 844. *et iam si animi natura* etc. *sentit, postquam de n. corp. distractast.* An assumption which Lucr. would not of course admit.

845. "it is nothing...". comptu: cf. I. 950 (Passage 2).

851. repetentia: a Lucretian word. "The recollection of our former selves."

852. et nunc, "so too now" we have no care about past selves (*illis*).

861. Cf. l. 924: *longe ab sensiferis primordia motibus errant.* The atoms which produce sensation have still been in motion, but being no longer in the body they have not been producing sensation.
deerrarunt: trisyllable.
862. Lucr. now resumes the main thread of his argument which he dropped at l. 843 to deal with two parenthetical suppositions (ll. 843–846 and 847–861). *enim* refers not to what immediately precedes but to the passage ending at l. 842. misere futurumst: cf. *male est, bene est.*
863. esse, "exist".
864. probet = *prohibet*: cf. *praebere* from *praehibere.*
865. "upon whom ills might be brought".
868. an nullo: an elliptic constr., supply *utrum aliquo tempore.*
870. *se ipsum indignari.* A personal acc. after *indignari* is rare in place of *casum suum.* Here a second acc. (of the thing) follows, namely the *fore ut* clause. "Lament his lot, that...".
871. posto = *posito*, "laid away".
872. interfiat: pass. of *interficere.*
873. "he does not ring true", i.e. his professed belief in the mortality of the soul (ll. 874, 875) does not ring true.
874. caecum cordi stimulum, "a secret pang". See Intro. p. xx.
876. "he does not grant what he professes nor the ground for his profession": neither the absence of sensation after death nor the reasons for this (which Lucr. has just been discussing).
877. eicit, disyllable (cf. Virgil, *Ecl.* III. 96: *reice capellas*).
878. esse...super = *superesse.*
879. vivus, "in life".
881. miseret, usually impers., *misereri* being used with a personal subj. illim = *illinc*, i.e. *ab illo corpore.*
882, 883. "thinks that it is he", *illum* being attracted from *illud* (sc. *corpus*).
885. "no other self".
888. nam, explaining his mention of flames (*uri*) as well as wild beasts (*lacerari*). The ordinary rites of burial would be as bad as any violence done to the body after death.
889. qui, abl.

894 ff. Men say (*aiunt*, l. 898).

896. **praeripere**, "be the first to snatch": inf. of purpose after verb of motion, *occurrent*.

897. **factis florentibus esse**: abl. of accompanying circumstances, "be in prosperity".

901. **unā**: together with what? Perhaps with Giuss. read *ullum*.

904 ff. Lucr. has just shown that the dead cannot feel any regret; he now goes on to say that the living have no cause to feel regret on the dead man's behalf.

906. **prope**, "near at hand".

909. **ab hoc**, the last speaker.

914. **ex animo**, "from the heart". **hic**, pron.

915. **iam fuerit**, lit. "already it shall have been" (and be no more), i.e. "soon it is past".

916. "this is to be the chief of their ills": *hoc mali* together.

917. **sitis**, in contrast to the plentiful supply of drink at the feast. **torrat** = *torreat*: transferred conjugation as though from *torrēre*. A conjectural reading is *torres*, "drought".

918. **aliae**: early Latin form of gen. **rei**: monosyllable (but spondee II. 112).

919 ff. In sleep we do not feel the lack of consciousness: still less in death.

921. **per nos**, "for all we care".

924. See n. to l. 861.

929. **leto**, "by means of death", "through death".

930. **secuta est**, "has overtaken".

931. **rerum natura**, personified as often elsewhere in the *de R.N.*

933. **quid** etc., "why is death (understood from the emphatic *mortalis*) so great a matter to you (with *tantoperest*, cf. l. 862 and n.), that...?"

935. **si**: "Nature" catches us on the horns of a dilemma, *si*... being followed by *sin*... (l. 940).

936. **pertusum...vas**: the phrase is no doubt suggested by the story of the Danaids.

940. **quae...cumque**: acc. with *fruor, fungor* not uncommon in early Latin. Cf. l. 956.

941. **in offensa est**, "is a stumbling-block".

944, 945. Nature can offer us no novelty "there is no new thing under the sun" (Ecclesiastes i. 9).

946. si begins a second dilemma. The dissatisfied man is either young and because there is nothing new should be content to die (ll. 946–951); or he is old and, having wasted his life, should be equally content to die (ll. 952–963). Nature's speech breaks off and is taken up again in the middle of the dilemma.

954. inclamet, sc. *natura.*

955. abhinc, either = *hinc*, "from here", or, in a temporal sense, "henceforth". Both meanings are rare, the normal meaning being "ago", looking from the present to the past, not to the future. balatro (connected with vb. *blatero*), "babbler".

961. aliena tua aetate, "unfitted to your years". tamen, although not *satur*.

962. agedum and *age* make an imperative more emphatic.

963. agat, t.t. of the law-court, "plead". incilet archaic = *increpet.*

966. No man goes to a world below: he is needed elsewhere, as we see in the grim line that follows.

967. materies, nom. opus is predicate: a common constr. in Lucr.

969. haec = *saecla* in general, not *postera saecla.* ante, adv.

971. A memorable use of legal terminology: life is not given for freehold (*mancipio*) but only on lease (*usu*). The case of both nouns is either abl. of manner, or pred. dat. (*usui* contracted).

972. Lucr. returns to the thought of the opening lines of the passage, 832 ff.

973. *ante quam nascimur.*

974. The past is mirror to the future.

977. omni, as often after a comp. = "any".

20. III. 59–93

59 ff. The connection between avarice and ambition and the fear of death is not at once obvious: see the running commentary at the end of this passage.

61. "and sometimes as accomplices...".

65. ferme, as often in Lucr., "for the most part".

66. stabili, a key-word in this passage: man's desire is ever for something firm and sure amid the fleeting impermanence of his daily life.

67. "loiter already on the threshold of death".

68. unde (with **effugisse**)=*a contemptu et egestate*. **se** is subj. of *effugisse*.

69. **remosse**: as obj. understand either *ea* (from *unde*), or perhaps *se*.

70. **rem conflant**, "amass riches".

73. **consanguineum**: gen. plur. mensas, because of possible poison.

74. ab eodem...timore, sc. *mortis*.

78. partim=*nonnulli*. ergo=*causâ*.

83. hunc, sc. *timorem*. pudorem (obj. of *vexare*), "honour".

87–93 = II. 55–61 and VI. 35–41. It is a passage which sums up Lucr.'s mission.

21. I. 136–145

136. animi fallit: see n. on I. 922 (Passage 2).

137–139. Lucr. makes a similar complaint in two other places, I. 830 ff. and III. 258 ff. Cicero took a different view and maintained that Latin was a better language than Greek (he probably meant contemporary Greek) for philosophy. The real difficulty lay in turning Greek philosophy into Latin *poetry* (*Latinis versibus*).

142. noctes vigilare serenas etc.: a rare personal touch. We may picture the poet-philosopher gazing up at the *noctis signa severa* while he hammered out the lines in which the laws of the universe were set forth.

INDICES

TO THE
INTRODUCTION, RUNNING COMMENTARY, AND NOTES

Reference is to pages

I. GENERAL

(Only those subjects are indexed to which the reader cannot easily refer by consulting the list of contents.)

II. LATIN WORDS AND PHRASES

(This index is intended to cover the more important points treated in the notes.)

regere imperio, 127
religio, 109

semina rerum, 106
severa, 129
simulacra, 121, 123
subus, 125
suffire, 131

tempore puncto, 116
thyrsus, 109

utilitas, 126
utqui, 131

velle, 125
vermina, 125

For a full Index to the *de R.N.* the reader is referred to
J. Paulson's Index (2nd ed. Göteborg, 1926).

For EU product safety concerns, contact us at Calle de José Abascal, 56–1°,
28003 Madrid, Spain or eugpsr@cambridge.org.

www.ingramcontent.com/pod-product-compliance
Ingram Content Group UK Ltd.
Pitfield, Milton Keynes, MK11 3LW, UK
UKHW020315140625
459647UK00018B/1878